Critical Success Factors Simplified

Implementing the Powerful Drivers of Dramatic Business Improvement

Critical Success Factors Simplified

Implementing the Powerful Drivers of Dramatic Business Improvement

Marvin T. Howell

CRC Press
Taylor & Francis Group
Boca Raton   London   New York

CRC Press is an imprint of the
Taylor & Francis Group, an **informa** business

A PRODUCTIVITY PRESS BOOK

Productivity Press
Taylor & Francis Group
270 Madison Avenue
New York, NY 10016

Library of Congress Cataloging-in-Publication Data

Howell, Marvin T., 1936-
    Critical success factors simplified : implementing the powerful drivers of dramatic business improvement / Marvin T. Howell.
        p. cm.
    Includes bibliographical references and index.
    ISBN 978-1-4398-1117-7
    1. Organizational effectiveness--Measurement. 2. Performance--Measurement. 3. Performance standards. 4. Total quality management. 5. Business planning. I. Title.

    HD58.9.H693 2010
    658.4'013--dc22   2009028125

Visit the Taylor & Francis Web site at
http://www.taylorandfrancis.com

and the Productivity Press Web site at
http://www.productivitypress.com

Contents

Preface

It's a rare business that doesn't incorporate critical-to-success factors (CSFs) into its strategic plan. Unfortunately, it's equally rare for organizations to take full advantage of the potential of CSFs to drive their organizational initiatives and processes.

Certainly, CSFs are extraordinarily popular. A Google search on November 22, 2008, showed 9.7 million examples of CSFs, from projects to business, to software, to automobiles, and more. In this book, I'll teach you how to identify and select CSFs for initiatives, how to measure their impact, and how to take corrective action when necessary. Whether you're a manager in an organization, a team member, or a process owner, this book is for you. Success is not often accomplished without a plan and knowledge of the factors that you need to address in order to accomplish your objective.

Why a book solely on CSFs? Because CSFs are *that* important. It's no exaggeration to say that they can be transformative, for your organization and for your personal and professional lives.

Although the Internet and the occasional article can give you an overview of CSFs, no other resource offers a simple, straightforward process for identifying and monitoring your CSFs—and making real-time changes to impact your bottom line.

In this book, you'll learn how to identify, measure, and use CSFs to successfully implement strategic plans, programs, and systems, manage projects, and improve processes and jobs. This book is the first to give you a simple process to track progress, highlight problem areas, and facilitate improvements. Whether you're trying to increase productivity, improve customer service, or even launch your own business, following the process in this book can help you turn *any* venture into a successful venture.

The book is organized into two parts. In the first part, I'll give you a background on CSFs, outline Rockart's CSF method, show you two powerful techniques for identifying external CSFs, and demonstrate a simple process for generating internal CSFs. I also present a road map for creating an organization-wide CSF program. In the second part of the book, we'll cover specific applications of CSFs, from strategic planning to individual pursuits.

If you're ready to maximize the use of CSFs in your organization and in your life, read on.

Chapter 1

Introduction

Since 1961, organizations have relied on critical-to-success factors (CSFs) to define the things that must go right—whether a system, program, project, process, or job—if their organizations are to achieve their purpose, mission, or objective.

CSFs can be used at all levels of an organization—from management on down to the trenches. They can stem from internal improvement initiatives, such as a need to improve workplace efficiency, or originate from external forces—changes in technology, legislation, or a stealth attack from the competition. You can use CSFs for strategic planning, to implement a system or program, or to manage a project, process, job, or even an individual pursuit.

CSFs' potential is virtually limitless, but, as is true of any tool, they're only as effective as their implementation. To be genuinely effective, CSFs need to be part of a planning process, a management system, production or program goals, or a specific individual pursuit. And identifying CSFs is only the first step. Once you know which factors are critical to your organization's success, you need to determine how to ensure top performance on those factors and measure progress and make adjustments as needed. In this book, I'll teach you how to do all of these things: how to identify your own critical-to-success factors, use them to measure your progress toward your goals, and take corrective action when needed.

If you follow my process, I can guarantee that your CSFs won't sit on the shelf with the strategic or business plan. Instead, they'll drive you to dramatic improvement and breakthrough performance.

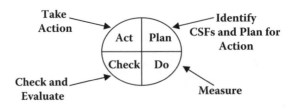

Figure 1.1   The Deming wheel or cycle.

Why use CSFs? Here are just a few of the advantages:

1. CSFs are simple to understand.
2. They focus attention on concerns and factors critical to the success of the initiative—regardless of what that initiative may be.
3. They can be a part of the strategic planning process, system, or program implementation, improving or reengineering a process, improving job performance, or driving an individual pursuit.
4. They're easy to monitor, and the benefits are significant.

A significant benefit to implementing CSFs is that they're drivers, not initiatives in their own right: in other words, they can be used to enhance, rather than supplant, organizational improvement initiatives already in place. As an example, let's take a look at how CSFs relate to the Deming wheel of continuous improvement: plan-do-check-act (Figure 1.1).

As you can see in Figure 1.1, for every stage of the Deming wheel, there is a corresponding phase of CSF implementation.

Rockart's Four Types of CSFs

According to Rockart,[1] there are four types of CSFs: industry (factors specific to a particular industry); strategic (factors specific to an organization's particular strategy, developed for competitive advantage); environmental (external influences, such as technology advancements, the economy, and political or regulatory actions); and temporal (factors arising from short-term situations and forces internal to an organization). A successful organization-wide CSF program will incorporate all four CSF types. Here are some examples of each of the four types:

Industry
- Increase customer retention to 95% or higher
- Answer telephone in three rings
- Decrease cost of poor quality (COPQ) by 10% this year
- Achieve next-day delivery of furniture
- Price match
- Increase customer satisfaction from satisfied to very satisfied by year-end 2008

Strategy
- Provide Six Sigma quality by end of 2009
- Improve process performance by 10% in next twelve months
- Become the lowest-priced provider of service
- Introduce 75% of product line in the last five years
- Deliver package by 10:30 a.m. tomorrow

Environmental
- Raise CD rates by 4% by April this year
- Raise interest rate by 10% by end of the year
- Lower cost of capital by 3%
- Raise copy rate by 15% with new copier
- Increase production by 50% per month with new improved machinery

Temporal
- Decrease absentee rate to 3% or less each year
- Decrease number of spills of hazardous materials in shop area to zero every year
- Increase employee satisfaction to 98% or higher; "very satisfied" on our annual employee satisfaction survey
- Decrease employee turnover rate to less than 5% a year
- Increase by 10% a year the number of processes that are in statistical control and stable
- Decrease cycle time by 20% this fiscal year
- Decrease rework from 20% to less than 5% at our construction site this year

Let's take a look at how these four CSF types might fit within a typical organizational hierarchy (Figure 1.2).

If you're in top management at your organization, your job description likely includes goals and objectives attainment. You'll need to pay attention to all four types of CSFs. Strategy is the name of your game, and all of your organizational CSFs will likely be incorporated into your strategic or

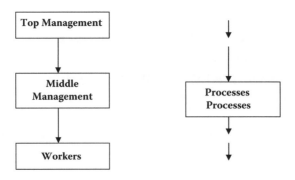

Figure 1.2   Hierarchies.

business plan. If you're in middle management, your CSFs will likely include the environmental and temporal categories, and possibly some industry CSFs. First-line supervisors and workers need to pay attention to temporal and environmental CSFs—often the CSFs with the most immediate impact on the work at hand. The point to take away here is that CSFs are important across *all* levels of your organization.

Categorizing CSFs

CSFs can be loosely grouped into three categories, which we'll call A, B, and C (Figure 1.3). The type of CSF you'll be implementing depends on the type of initiative you're undertaking (Figure 1.4).

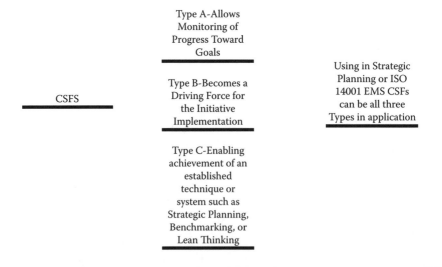

Figure 1.3   CSF types (A, B, and C).

Strategic planning (*type B accompanied by type A*): See Chapter 5.

System (*type A*): See Chapter 6.

Program (*type A accompanied by type B or C*): See Chapter 7.

Project (*type A accompanied by type C*).

Process (*Type C*): See Chapter 8.

Job (*Type C*): See Chapter 9.

Individual (*Type B accompanied by type A*): See Chapter 10.

Figure 1.4 Initiatives by type(s).

Goals or Objectives → CSFs → Measures and Targets → Actions to Achieve → Targets and Success of Action → Monitor ↓

Figure 1.5 CSF achievement model made simple.

Objective CSFs—Measure—Monitor—Take action

Figure 1.6 CSF achievement model made even simpler.

In later chapters, I'll walk you through the model for identifying and measuring CSFs, taking action, and monitoring your progress. But first, let's take a look at the general and simplified models for implementing and tracking CSFs (Figures 1.5 and 1.6).

In Chapter 4, we'll go into this model in more detail, and provide you with the measurement tools that you'll need to make your CSFs more effective. For now, just keep in mind that your CSFs need to be directly related to your objectives, that implementation without monitoring is not enough, and that not all CSFs are created equal: some will be more critical to your organization's success than others.

Why Should You Implement CSFs in Your Organization?

Using CSFs is a top-down management approach and technique that enables success in an organization's improvement efforts. It provides excellent focus for beginning the implementation of an improvement activity or program. Implementing CSFs in an organization will:

1. Reduce the risk of failure in business and strategic objectives attainment

2. Further the understanding of management as to what it takes to successfully implement a strategic plan or a major change initiative
3. Achieve an increased employee buy-in to programs, systems, or process improvements
4. Increase dramatically the use of this value-added technique in planning, developing, and implementing programs, systems, process improvements, and operational enhancements
5. Facilitate continuous improvement of operations and process performance

Getting Started

We've talked about what CSFs are, why they're important to your organization, and have given you a glimpse of how they can be organized and categorized. Before we dive in to identifying, tracking, and measuring progress, however, a word of caution is in order: while CSFs have the power to transform your improvement initiatives, your organization, and even your personal life, they aren't a magic bullet, and simply identifying one or two corporate CSFs isn't likely to get you where you need to go.

The notion of *corporate CSFs* originated in the 1980s. Generally implemented as a strategy CSF, corporate CSFs were driven by the belief that locating that one or two critical factors and achieving those would ensure organizational success and sustainability. This is how the corporate CSF approach usually played out: management analysts went to various offices, interviewed key people or held workshop, and gathered what they thought was crucial information. The factors that they came up with were screened by management as to whether they satisfied the following criteria:

1. Had an overall impact on key performance measures
2. Had an obvious relationship to the strategic direction and issues of the organization
3. Had a relationship to or impact on important business activities
4. Showed a relationship to stages or organizational life cycle, such as introduction, beginning, growth, or decline
5. Impacted large amounts of capital and resources

Corporate CSFs were vigorously pursued in part because of the tremendous success of FedEx in achieving timely delivery of packages, way ahead of any competitor. But here's where the conventional wisdom was off target:

companies assumed that this "corporate CSF" (timely delivery of packages) led FedEx to a competitive advantage. Though timely delivery *could* be labeled a CSF, it was actually Fred Smith's *vision* for FedEx: "We will deliver your package by 10:30 tomorrow morning." Fred Smith brought his vision to fruition by making it a centerpiece of all employees' day-by-day plans and actions. His vision *drove* his CSFs: his planning system, improvement actions, leadership, employee buy-in, and focused efforts. Fred Smith's approach clearly included so much more than simply identifying a corporate CSF and deploying it as a corporate or strategic thrust. Decades later, FedEx is still going strong.

Breakthroughs such as FedEx's can result even today, through strategic planning or policy deployment. CSFs can help you achieve your vision, goals, objectives, and strategies. Measurement, action plans, and executive reviews, along with CSFs, are powerful enablers in achieving dramatic business success. But simply identifying a corporate CSF and achieving it does not necessarily lead to success. CSFs can *help* to do that when used to implement an improvement initiative efficiently and effectively. To survive in today's competitive global economy, you need a full toolkit of strategies. CSFs belong in *every* organization's toolkit. In the following chapters, I'll show you how you can use CSFs to undergird your organization's processes, initiatives, and strategies.

Chapter 2

Identifying CSFs: External CSFs

Before you can effectively use CSFs to impact your organization, you need to identify them. Simply put, what are the factors that are absolutely critical to your success? In Chapter 2, we'll talk about how to identify external CSFs: factors beyond your immediate control that can have a huge impact on your success. Later, in Chapter 3, we'll look at internal CSFs and dive into the CSF method.

All organizations are impacted by external forces. These forces can come from several sources, such as national, state, or local government regulations and taxes, to social work ethics, to demographics. External CSFs can have either a negative or positive impact, but the negative impacts can be lessened if your organization anticipates and prepares for them. An environmental scan can help you identify these external CSFs.

Environmental Scan

An environmental scan is just what it sounds like: a deliberate accounting of the factors that will potentially influence your business and the CSFs that will drive your strategic plan. Although your scan can be conducted by a specific section or department within your organization, ideally you'll want to convene a cross-functional team, or a team of members representing the major functional areas of your business, such as marketing, production, engineering, and administration. Because external CSFs can have a significant impact on your strategic plan, and your plan represents the entire organization, all major functions should be represented and have a voice in the plan's development—and identifying external CSFs needs to be part of that development. You can convene your team by asking for volunteers within each group, which generally gives you a high degree of buy-in, or by asking for recommendations from the head of each department or function and assigning team members.

Your team will look at a number of different factors while conducting the scan, such as:

1. Government
   - Legislation coming in next few years
   - Regulations, such as environmental, distribution, traveling, etc.
   - Taxes—State income, rise in sales taxes, business taxes, etc.
   - Support—Possible support received to business
2. Industry
   - Market volume
   - Market share or pricing
   - Energy supply and reliability
   - Supply capacity
3. Economy
   - Possible inflation
   - Expected wage levels
   - What the labor supply (professionals, workers) will be
4. Technology
   - What new technology is expected
   - How it will affect various processes/industries
   - Productivity increases
   - Maintenance and life cycle costs
5. Social
   - Work ethics
   - Demographics changes
   - Ecology
   - Consumer protection

Evaluating the Findings

Once you've conducted your environmental scan, you'll need to evaluate the findings.

Your cross-functional team, either alone or in conjunction with top management at a strategic planning session, can conduct the evaluation. The following exercise will help your team identify the CSFs most important to your organization's strategic plan.

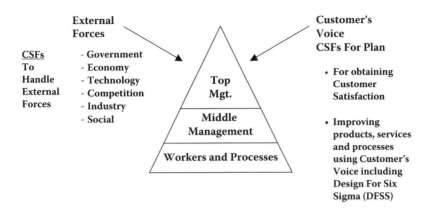

Figure 2.1 Environmental scan.

Hox and Majiluf[2] developed a profile chart to help evaluate the findings of an environmental scan. They suggested that each critical external factor be graded on a five-point scale:

++ Extremely attractive
+ Mildly attractive
E Even or neutral
– Mildly unattractive
= Extremely unattractive

Figure 2.1 shows an example of an environmental scan.

The profile makes visible which critical external factor(s) to consider in the organization's strategic planning process. As you'd expect, the mildly unattractive and extremely unattractive factors will have a negative impact on the company or organization.

In the example in Figure 2.1, taxes, labor supply, and wage levels are unfavorable, while the market, energy supply, and productivity are favorable. The CSF(s) selected will depend on management's perspective on the course of action or strategy the organization should pursue. For example, they might try to increase market share by introducing new products, or improve organizational quality and productivity through implementing Lean and Six Sigma. These different objectives would call for different CSFs.

Once you've identified your external CSFs, it's up to your organization's management to prepare for them. In Figure 2.2, the customer voice and external forces have the arrow pointing at top management.

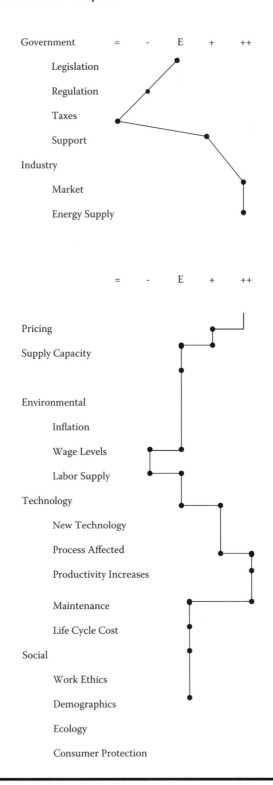

Figure 2.2 External forces.

Both the customer voice and external forces affect all three levels of the hierarchy (as you'll recall from Chapter 1, the levels include top management, middle management, and first-line supervisors/workers), but it is top management that must understand them and factor the essential information into their strategic planning efforts. One way to do this is through a SWOT analysis.

SWOT Analysis

One tool to have in your arsenal as you begin to identify objectives for your strategic planning process is a SWOT analysis. In a SWOT analysis, *S* stands for *strengths*, *W* for *weaknesses*, *O* for *opportunities*, and *T* for *threats*. Again, your SWOT analysis will be formulated by a team using a brainstorming (see Appendix B) or nominal group technique (see Appendix C) to generate possibilities under each of these four categories. After you've generated your list of items, you need to clarify, consolidate, add to, change, and ultimately, finalize it. Once you've articulated these factors, strengths can be used to overcome threats and weaknesses, or to take advantage of opportunities. Figure 2.3 shows a mini-SWOT.

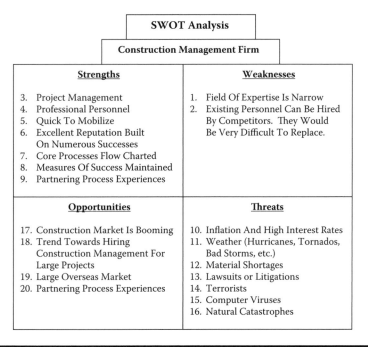

Figure 2.3   SWOT analysis.

Let's take some strengths and match them against opportunities. First, let's look at (5) quick to mobilize (strength) versus (19) large overseas market. In this instance, the organization should create a strategic objective to break into or extend market share in overseas market. Next, let's look at strength (9), partnering, versus threat (13), litigation. Partnering helps minimize the chance of litigation. Therefore, mobilization and partnering both could be considered strategic objectives. The CSFs selected will vary by the strategy selected. Mobilization would require mobilization planning, competent personnel willing to relocate, and a market strategy. Partnering CSFs will include bringing all parties together, conducting meetings to facilitate the process, reaching a mutually acceptable agreement, and formalizing a potential conflict process.

Large businesses might identify many external forces within each category. Once identified and evaluated, these external forces will help you develop and implement your strategic objectives. You'll then need to move on to developing performance measures and action plans. In most cases, you can't control the external CSFs that impact your business. However, you do need to attend to them if you don't want to either be adversely affected or miss a great opportunity. Although your strategic plan should be developed, at least in part, based on *external* CSFs, the plan's implementation and success will be driven by your *internal* CSFs. In Chapter 3, we'll discuss how to identify the internal CSFs that will be critical to achieving your strategic objectives.

Chapter 3

Identifying CSFs: Internal CSFs

In Chapter 2, we discussed external CSFs—the factors critical to your organization's success that are, for the most part, beyond your immediate control. But there are other CSFs, internal CSFs, that are always present *within* your organization, whether you identify and use them or not. These CSFs can enable your organization's success, helping you attain major, organization-wide goals and strategic objectives, or targeted goals for suborganizations, such as regions, business units, or divisions.

In this chapter, I'll explain how to identify the CSFs that can help your organization successfully tackle its goals and objectives. We'll start by examining Rockart's original CSF method.[3,2]

The Original CSF Method

The original CSF method is a step-by-step method for identifying CSFs; it is not an algorithm, however, in that no defined number of iterations will lead to an exact answer. Although articles, papers, and a primer have been written on this method, it can be complicated, and includes numerous requirement matrices, assumptions, and scenarios. Given adequate time and with the right people on board, the original CSF method can work for your organization. We'll discuss the original CSF method in the paragraphs below, followed by the five-phase CSF method. Later, we'll discuss a very simple method that can satisfy 90% of your applications needs.

According to Rockart, a pioneer and expert in the field of CSF development, the first step in implementing CSFs in your organization is to establish a compelling five- to twenty-year vision that everyone in the organization can strive toward, and to write a dynamic mission statement. Your mission statement should detail your organization's purpose and spell out why your organization exists. For example, a financial institution's mission statement may be to "develop financial management strategies that are beneficial and safe for our clients." Next, you'll need to develop five to six strategic objectives or goals for your organization. Make them SMART (specific, measurable, actionable, realistic and relevant, and time framed).

Third, place your objectives in a hierarchy, and stratify your objective to the activities or actions necessary to achieve it. Determine whether you've identified the right activities by asking yourself, "If these actions are successful, will my objective be achieved?" Next, ask: "What assumptions do I need to make so that this scenario is realistic and so that the CSFs identified are useful and meaningful?" Once your objectives and assumptions have been articulated, you'll be ready to identify possible CSFs.

Let's consider how this looks in practice. The following example illustrates the original CSF method. We'll walk through each of the above steps, from developing vision, to establishing objectives, to writing a mission statement, to validating your objectives and goals through your assumptions.

Example: A Construction Company

A horizontal and vertical construction company wants to improve productivity by 20% during their next large project, with a more than two-year project life. Management selected a three-year project for this strategic objective, and developed their vision, mission, and goals as shown in Figure 3.1.

The construction company then created an objective-to-requirements hierarchy diagram, which illustrates the series of activities that must be completed to achieve their specific objective. In the construction company's case, the hierarchy diagram will be used to ask questions, record assumptions, and ultimately, to determine whether their planned actions are likely to be adequate in meeting their goal of 20% increased productivity. Figure 3.2 shows a typical, but abbreviated, hierarchy diagram.

The construction company felt that its objective—to improve productivity by 20% over the course of three years—was a priority, and needed to be met to stay ahead of fierce competition for future similar projects. The three

MISSION STATEMENT

The *mission* of our Quality Construction Company is to design and build quality construction that meets client's expectations and at or below budget.

VISION STATEMENT

When you need a new facility, system, or any project, you first think of Quality Construction Company.

GOALS

Our goals are:

Provide quality construction every time
Always within budget
On or ahead of schedule
With world-class safety performance

Figure 3.1   Vision, mission, and goals.

questions illustrated in Figure 3.2 are typical and often relevant regardless of industry, but others may be more appropriate for your hierarchy.

Your first step in this process, then, is to record your objective(s). Next, annotate your assumptions and, from them, select your possible CSFs. Figure 3.3 demonstrates this technique.

Now, you'll need to evaluate your potential CSFs. For each one, ask: "Is this factor *critical* to the success of this objective? Can the objective be accomplished without this factor being achieved?" If the answer to the first question is no, then it is a CSF. Conversely, if you answer yes to the second question, then it is *not* a CSF. Using these two questions, a yes and no answer, respectively, will most probably identify a CSF vital to the objective's success. In this example, every CSF identified is confirmed as a CSF. They are truly critical to achieving the productivity objective.

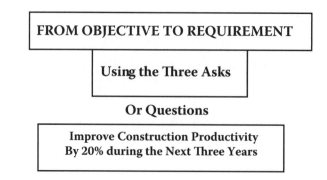

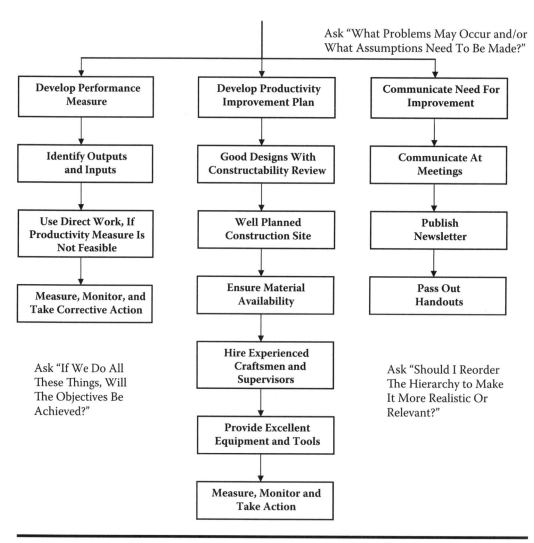

Figure 3.2 From objective to requirement.

GOING FROM OBJECTIVES TO ASSUMPTIONS
TO POTENTIAL CSFs

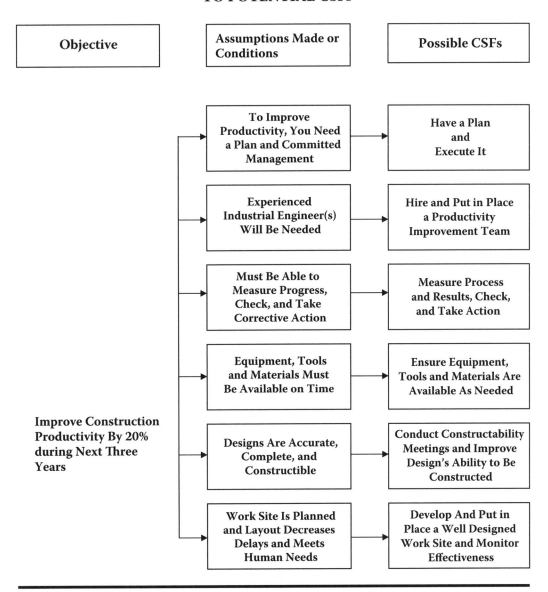

Figure 3.3   Going from objectives to assumptions to potential CSFs.

The Five-Phase CSF Method

A revised and more contemporary method for identifying CSFs, which evolved from the original CSF method, includes five distinct phases: scope, collecting data, evaluating and organizing data, identifying and selecting the CSFs, and analyzing and validating the CSFs.

Phase 1: Scope

During the scope phase, your task is to identify and define what needs to be done and determine who needs to do it. Is the CSF method being used for an organization or suborganization? Is it for a mission achievement or achieving strategic goals? Or is it for an improvement initiative such as Six Sigma, process improvement, Lean office, reengineering, etc.? Who should participate? For high-level CSFs, you'll want to convene a cross-functional team and identify a top management person as the champion, or person responsible, for the strategic objective. He or she will ensure that a competent, motivated team is formed to identify the CSFs and will put together a charter for the team. For lower-level CSFs, a cross-functional team might not be strictly necessary; in some cases, an individual can compile and present findings to a responsible executive or steering group or guiding team.

Phase 2: Collecting Data

To identify CSFs, you need to collect data. The two best techniques for collecting data are *reviewing documents* and *interviewing key personnel.*

Documents that should be reviewed include vision statements, mission statements, values and guiding principles, organizational strategies, strategic plan, department business plans, etc. So what are you looking for during your review of these documents? You want to find themes, key words, and relationships among key organizational initiatives (see Figure 3.4).

Interviews should be conducted one-on-one with key personnel, using already developed open-ended questions. Importantly, your interviews need to be conducted by someone who understands CSF development and use. Your interviewer will take notes during each interview and summarize them afterwards; later, your cross-functional team can evaluate the notes and organize them within a total data collection summary. When you're developing your interview questions, keep your objective(s) in mind. What do you need

The Relationship Diagram

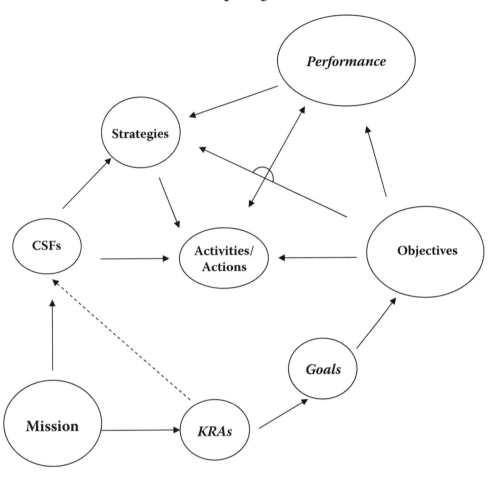

The Relationships (see glossary for definitions used) are shown below:

- **Mission drives CSFs and KRAs**
- **KRAs drive Goals**
- **Goals drive Objectives**
- **CSFs and Performance Measures drive Strategies**
- **CSFs drive Activities or Actions**
- **Objectives determine Performance Measures and Targets**
- **Strategies drive Actions or Activities**

Figure 3.4   The relationship diagram.

to know to meet that objective? You'll be looking for the answers in your interview questions. We'll discuss this process in more detail in phase 3.

Rockart's original CSF method suggests that the interview process consists of two to three sessions, each conducted at least one day apart. The first session is conducted with the general manager or executive to determine his or her goals or objectives and to discuss each and identify possible CSFs. In the second interview session, you'll again meet with the interviewee to review the first session's results and validate their completeness and adequacy. Holding the second session a few days after the first enables both the interviewer and the executive to consider the CSFs and revise or improve them if needed. Two interviews may be sufficient for finalizing the CSFs; in particularly complicated cases, however, a third session may be needed to finalize the CSFs and measures. Interviews with key personnel are time-consuming and can be expensive. But without them, it's unlikely that you can effectively implement, measure, and track CSFs within your organization.

Phase 3: Evaluate and Organize the Data

Your next step is to organize the data collected so that you can evaluate it for content and completeness. Begin by developing activity statements— statements detailing the activities or actions that you need to undertake, as suggested by the data. Write as many as the data support. Now, it is time to start narrowing down your activities and actions to what's important. This list will ultimately yield your CSFs.

What areas, or themes, do these activities represent? Use an affinity diagram to identify the different topic or subject areas that the activities seem to be associated with or similar to.[4] To use an affinity diagram, write each data finding on a sheet of paper or on 3 × 5 index cards. Place all of your cards on a flat surface, such as a table. Rearrange the cards into similar groupings. Once your groupings are completed, read each card within each grouping. On a separate card, write a theme that best describes each grouping. These header cards for each grouping are your themes. In other words, summary themes can be drawn from the clusters or topic areas identified from the data. These important themes are known as *key results areas* (KRAs). In step 3, we'll identify your CSFs from your KRAs. Not all KRAs will become CSFs: only those that are genuinely *critical* to achieving your objective.

Appendix A lists more than 40 of the most common KRAs for organizations, which vary by industry, market, location, and other factors. For utilities, for example, quality, cost, delivery, safety, and community relationships enable customer satisfaction. For FedEx, people, service, and profit drive both their strategic planning and their daily operations. Construction companies usually select quality, cost/budget, schedule, and safety as their KRAs. Table 3.1 shows these KRAs for our construction company and some of the activities (as identified through affinity diagramming) for each.

KRAs can be extremely useful for strategic planning. Generally speaking, resources applied to a KRA will pay the highest dividends. KRAs can be made into long-range, broad goals simply by adding an action word, such as *increase, improve, decrease, reduce*, etc. Short-term, specific objectives can then be identified that support the goals.

KRA statements need to be as brief as possible. No action verbs are allowed. They reflect results (outputs or outcomes), not actions.

Phase 4: Identify and Select the CSFs

From the KRAs, we'll identify and define our potential CSFs. Distinguishing between KRAs and CSFs can be confusing at best; the important thing to remember is that it is their *application* that distinguishes them. Here's the strategic linkage: vision–mission–KRAs–goals–CSFs–objectives–measures–action plans–implementation–executive or management reviews–corrective action. In other words, the goals that need to be met to achieve a KRA are identified, and the CSFs *drive* the actions needed to achieve these goals.

Figure 3.5 shows the relationships between KRAs and CSFs.

CSFs, then, are those factors critical to achieving success in an initiative or mission. CSFs are critical to achieving your organizational KRA. CSF implementation enables success of the KRAs, and, consequently, your organizational mission and vision. CSFs also drive objectives attainment.

CSF statements can range from a few words to a complete sentence, with a recommended length of ten words or less. This length is easier to remember or explain than lengthier CSF statements. CSF statements can detail either a desired activity or a desired result, such as top management commitment and employee buy-in. Table 3.2 shows criteria for a well-written CSF.

Phase 5: Analyzing and Validating CSFs

So you've collected and evaluated your data and have identified your CSFs? Now what? During phase 5, you can use a variety of techniques or tools to ensure that you've chosen the correct CSFs: in other words, that the formula "data + analysis = information" has been accomplished accurately, sufficiently,

Table 3.1   KRAs and Their Corresponding Activities

Key Results Areas	*Activities*
Quality	Reduce rework
	Meet specifications on all work
	Satisfy or exceed client's expectations
	Meet quality standards and specifications
	Have weekly or monthly management meetings and review project performance measures; take corrective action where needed
Cost/budget	Bring project in on or under budget
	Purchase least expensive parts, tools, materials, and equipment
	Keep cost of poor quality low
	Measure operational efficiency during work performance and develop plans for improvement
	Perform process improvements and methods improvements
	Use foremen delay surveys to identify delays and take action when possible
	Design and plan a well-laid-out construction site
	Develop an excellent partner contract (use partnering process to set objectives and identify how conflicts will be handled) in order to minimize litigation
	Provide training where needed to ensure acceptable performance
	Use performance measures to manage the project and take action if undesired trend occurs
	Achieve team synergy in staff and crews
	Recognize and reward achievement
	Have accurate and easy-to-retrieve information for decision making and communications
	Ensure that all roles and responsibilities are fully defined and communicated
Schedule	Schedule work weekly and adjust for daily work
	Use project management tools and techniques
	Measure earned value and use to manage project progress

Table 3.1 (continued)   KRAs and Their Corresponding Activities

Key Results Areas	Activities
Schedule (continued)	Order materials with long lead times in sufficient time to be ready when work is to be done
	Ensure adequate tools and equipment are on hand to accomplish work
	Identify critical path and slack time and use in scheduling
	Ensure designs are accurate, complete, and constructible
	Ensure crafts are coordinated and reduce any interference
	Hire experienced craftsmen, foremen, and supervisors
Safety	Develop and execute a safety program
	Benchmark other successful construction projects' safety programs and adopt best practices
	Management emphasizes safety at every opportunity
	Hold gang box safety meetings
	Have a full-time safety person when project is large enough
	Double-check scaffolding and other risky operations
	Communicate safety performance
	Investigate any accident or near accident, identify root cause(s), and foolproof method or activity to prevent any reoccurrence

and effectively. You can create *comparison matrices* to determine the relationships among your CSFs, KRAs, goals, objectives, values, etc., are understood. A *relationship diagram*[4] can also be very helpful in this endeavor. We'll go into these and other tools in more detail in the following chapters.

Once the CSFs and their relationships are fully understood, this phase has been completed. The CSFs identified for our construction project example with the productivity improvement objective are:

1. Hire, train, and motivate competent craftsmen, foremen, and supervisors.
2. Ensure designs are accurate, complete, and constructible.
3. Executives and managers are engaged and committed to project's objectives.
4. Provide sufficient resources–personnel, material, equipment, tools, and other requirements.

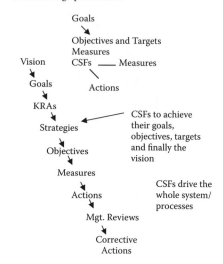

Figure 3.5   Relationships between KRAs and CSFs.

Table 3.2   Good and Poor CSF Criteria

Good	*Poor*
Clear: Easy to understand	Confusing: High word density and difficult to understand
Concise: Short—10 words or less	Lengthy: More than 10 words and hard to remember
Compelling content: Drives action	Not actionable: Does not encourage action
Correlated: When CSF is achieved, the objective is successful	Uncorrelated: CSF achieved, objective was not and vice versa.

5. Solve conflicts at the lowest level of the organization.

6. Measure key process performance, craftsmen performance, schedule performance, and safety performance; improve where needed and recognize and award achievements.

7. Meet all work specifications.

8. Achieve an acceptable productivity or operational efficiency of all work accomplished.

9. Emphasize safety and encourage safe work practices.
10. Measure earned value and use to manage the project's performance.

You need to ensure that at least one CSF is identified for each major theme or KRA. Here's how they fall in the construction example:

Quality
    7. Meet all work specifications.
    3. Executives and managers engaged and committed to project's objectives.
Cost
    4. Provide sufficient resources—personnel, material, equipment, tools, and other requirements.
    8. Achieve an acceptable productivity or operational efficiency of all work performed.
    5. Solve conflicts at the lowest level of the organization.
    6. Measure key process performance, craftsmen performance, schedule performance, and safety performance; improve where needed and recognize and award achievements.
Schedule
    1. Hire, train, and motivate competent craftsmen, foremen, and supervisors.
    2. Ensure designs are accurate, complete, and constructible.
    10. Measure earned value and use to manage the project's progress toward schedule achievement.
Safety
    9. Emphasize safety and encourage safe work practices.

Each of these areas is covered by at least one CSF. Ask yourself, "If these CSFs are achieved, will this KRA also be achieved?" Next, you need to ask, "If these CSFs are achieved, will the project's objective also be achieved?" If the answer is yes, then you have successfully identified the project's CSFs. If the answer is no, then you'll need to revisit the KRAs to determine whether any CSF was overlooked.

Some CSFs actually support more than one KRA. For example, CSF 1 supports both cost and schedule, CSF 10 both cost and schedule, CSF 7 both quality and cost, and so on. This kind of overlap is normal. In this example, the CSF was placed in the KRA it impacted the most. Some people prefer to illustrate the relationship by placing each CSF in all the KRAs it impacts or supports. Either way is okay.

Appendix E summarizes the five phases of the CSF method. These five phases, when followed, will enable you to identify and then select CSFs that are meaningful factors, genuinely critical to your success.

In Chapter 4, I'll expand on these methods and concepts to help you understand how you can use them in your initiatives to determine your degree of CSF implementation and success.

A Simple but Effective Method

At the beginning of this chapter, I promised to give you a simple, yet very effective, CSF method that can take care of 90% of your CSF identification needs. I'm not sure where this method first originated, but it's a generally practiced technique often used to generate ideas. I've added my own spin to this to make it more easy to use in identifying and selecting CSFs.

Let's say that a team is developing a strategic plan, business plan, or improvement initiative. Once the objectives with targets are identified, we're ready to launch our simple method.

Step 1. Make the objectives and targets visible to the team (on a blackboard, whiteboard, pad on an easel, etc.).

Step 2. Generate ideas for CSFs that are potentially pertinent to the initiative's implementation, and list where visible to the team members. Your team can brainstorm possible CSFs; for an even simpler approach, have your team review the traditional list of CSFs in Appendix D and select the ones that are applicable to your organization. Your team can then brainstorm to identify additional, organization-specific factors. The team does not have to go in any particular order, but each member can simply speak up as ideas are formulated in his or her mind.

Step 3. Evaluate each factor identified by asking, "Is this factor critical to the successful implementation of the initiative?" Write yes or no by the factor. The yes answers are your critical success factors.

Too simple? For some initiatives, yes, but this approach can often identify the factors critical for an initiative's success. It can be described as (1) knowing your objectives, (2) generating the possible factors, and (3) evaluating the criticality of the factors. The following example illustrates the simple method.

First Energy Company	
Vision	To be the best provider of electricity to our region and first on our customers' minds when additional energy is needed
Mission	Generate, transmit, and distribute electricity to our customers in the lowest price ever
KRAs	Quality, cost, delivery, safety, stakeholder satisfaction
Goals	Increase quality of our meter reading personnel
Objectives	Decrease meter reading errors by 5% in 2009
Measures	Number of meter reading errors/total meters × 100

Possible CSF (Brainstorming List)	Critical: Yes or No	Remarks
1. "How to read accurately" training to include field verification	No	Need to identify who needs the training. Training those who are not making errors could be morale lowering. Training some may be part of the solution.
2. Get new type of meter that is easier to read	No	Should be able to read present meters. Too costly to get meters for 5 million customers.
3. Employee (meter reader) involvement	Yes	Should be motivated, willing to learn and improve.
4. Measured and communicated at short time intervals	Yes	Without measurement, you don't know how you're doing and if your countermeasures are working.
5. Employ quality control	No	A random QC effort at first may be helpful, but way too expensive to deploy at all times.
6. Get scope for meter readers to read difficult-to-get-to meters from a distance	Maybe	Probably already done. Check. If so, don't put on the critical list.
7. Incentive program rewarding accuracy	No	Could be part of the solution
8. Customers' perception of accuracy	No, not to this specific objective	Could be that the customers don't feel this is a problem. If they don't, then get a new objective.
9. Analyze errors to discover root cause and develop corrective actions to eliminate them	Yes	Analysis as to who is making the errors and why is critical to reducing the errors. By knowing this, corrective action can be taken.

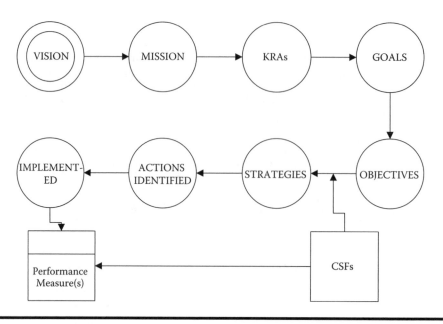

Figure 3.6   CSF relationships.

The three identified CSFs met the criticality question: "Is this factor critical to achieving the objective?" They were employee involvement, measurement, and analysis and corrective action. Figure 3.6 illustrates the flow of the above process and shows that the CSFs influence the objectives, their strategies, and actions taken; if they are met, then the results will be very successful. Figure 3.6 is similar to Figure 3.5, except that it shows the direct impact on the objective performance measure (sometimes referred to as key performance indicator (KPI)).

Next, First Energy's team needs to consider each objective for all of the organization's KRAs and identify the CSFs needed to make them happen. Finally, the team will need to determine how the CSFs' progress will be measured (we'll talk about this in more detail in Chapter 4), identify actions to improve the objective measure, implement the CSFs, and track their progress and results toward the objective. By continually tracking and monitoring your CSFs, you can immediately take corrective action if you go off course.

Again, in more than 90% of all situations where CSFs are needed to drive achievement, the simple approach demonstrated above will work very well. For more abstract problems or systems in which you have little available data at the outset, Rockart's original method for identifying CSFs may provide more insight into relationships, assumptions, risks, and potential CSFs.

Chapter 4

The CSF Achievement Model

In the prior chapters, we discussed what CSFs are, how they differ from KRAs, and how to begin the process of identifying the factors that are critical to your organization's success. In this chapter, we'll go into more detail on identifying and selecting appropriate CSFs, measuring their implementation progress, and deciding when and how to take corrective action.

First, let's flowchart the complete process, as shown in Figure 4.1.

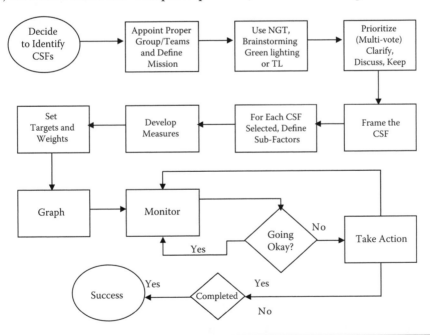

Figure 4.1   Process flowchart for creating and managing CSFs.

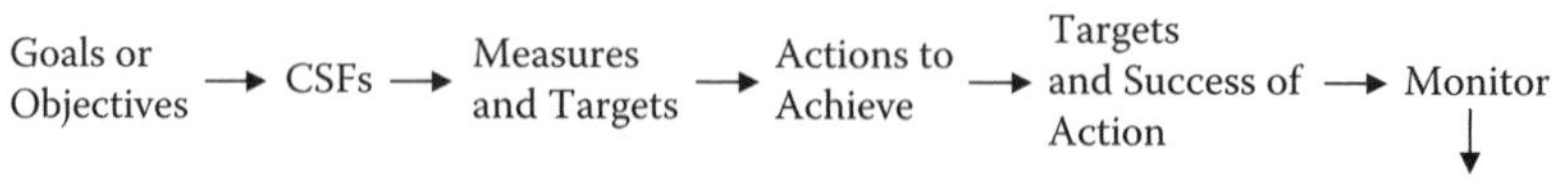

Goals or Objectives → CSFs → Measures and Targets → Actions to Achieve → Targets and Success of Action → Monitor ↓

Figure 4.2   CSF achievement model.

Figure 4.2 highlights a portion of the process called the *CSF achievement model*. This model, first mentioned in Chapters 2 and 3, will be demonstrated in detail in this chapter, and its use is the key thrust of this book. The model includes the modified five-step CSF method for identifying CSFs and extends to measuring the CSFs' implementation progress, monitoring, and taking corrective action if needed.

To use CSFs to help manage the implementation of a strategic plan, system, program, project, process, or an individual initiative, you need to follow a simple six-step process.

First, to prepare to use the model, you must commit to its use. You should follow the six defined steps. You should have already determined the improvement application you wish to use this process to achieve. The application can be strategic planning, systems development, a program, a process, a project, or an individual pursuit.

Once you've decided to use the process, you'll likely need a team to implement it. (For small initiatives, an individual can easily implement the method.) Form an appropriate team and charter it with a mission and goals. The type of team selected will depend on what they are expected to achieve. For example, a strategic plan could call for a cross-functional team, and implementing ISO 9001 or 14001 would require a cross-functional development team. Improving a workstation design would call for team members that perform that function (a functional team or natural work team). For an individual initiative, the team, of course, is a team of one, the individual.

Your mission, typically developed by top management, is simply what the team is tasked with accomplishing. In other words, the mission is the new team's reason for being. The team's goals are defined as the activities that they're expected to accomplish within a specific time frame. Now you are ready for step 1.

Step 1: Define the Goals or Objective of the Initiative You Wish to Achieve

Your first step is the most basic: for your improvement initiative, spell out specifically what you want to accomplish and when you want to have it done.

Steps 2 and 3: Identify and Select Your CSFs

Identifying (second step) and selecting (third step) CSFs is made easy since most management systems, reengineering processes, strategic planning, etc., have in common the same drivers or critical factors that need to be achieved for the initiative to be successful. These factors, which will be identified later in this step, are called a *traditional list* (TL) of CSFs. If the critical success factors for the initiative are not on the traditional list, teams should generate possible CSFs using brainstorming, green lighting (when the ideas from brainstorming are almost exhausted, the facilitator opens up the process to let anyone suggest a new idea), or the modified nominal group technique (a technique in which a group silently lists ideas, after which the facilitator goes around the room and lets everyone in sequence offer an idea). The ideas are listed on a pad or whiteboard so that they are visible to the group, after which they are discussed, combined, and prioritized.

Selecting the CSFs from the suggestions generated can be done by using multivoting, in which the team winnows down the list of CSFs through a series of votes. First, your team will select half of the CSFs on your full list—those that they feel are critical if your endeavor is to be successful. In each round of voting, you'll continue to select half of the factors on the list, until your list has been reduced to three to nine CSFs. Working with this manageable number of CSFs, your team will then need to discuss their criticality and compare them with predetermined criteria to identify the ones that they feel are pertinent.

Although this is not a consensus process, multivoting makes team members feel that their selection and perspective are valuable. For some technical improvement programs, pertinent factors specific to that industry or endeavor should be added to the identified CSFs in the traditional list. For other technical improvement initiatives, list the key processes or functions and then ask, "What is critical for me to accomplish my objective?" These two paths are shown in Figure 4.3.

Technical CSFs are things that may have to be built, developed, or furnished to achieve the CSF. A call center, a marketing strategy, a customer database with each customer profile, a new office building, added machinery, and new labor skills are examples. Sometimes, the organization may not be able to meet these and a lesser CSF may have to be selected.

Step 4: Determine Subfactors for Each Selected CSF

Write down a CSF on a whiteboard or a pad on an easel. Let the team discuss and identify subfactors that comprise the CSF. This exercise helps the

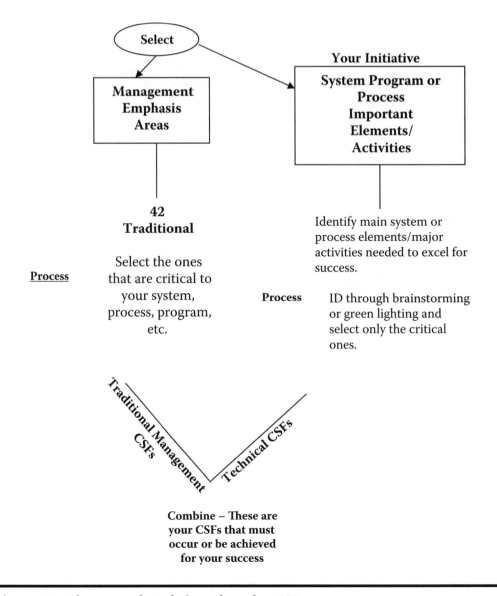

Figure 4.3   The two paths to being selected as CSFs.

team better understand the CSF and helps to determine how to measure its implementation. For example, write *quality* on the board or pad. Have the team list the most pertinent components, aspects, or subfactors.

Quality
- – Improve quality
- – Decrease rework
- – Increase process quality Sigma level
- – Decrease cost of quality

A Call Center Example

Often, companies will find they must meet some of the traditional list CSFs, plus some technical requirements or needs specific to the initiative or endeavor. Which of the TL CSFs apply? Top management commitment, resources, employee involvement, and training are good possibilities.

To further explain the first four steps, let's look at a call center example, outlining seven possible measures for tracking CSFs' progress. Our call center has formed a team to improve production, or the total number of calls handled effectively in an eight-hour shift, by 10%.

To function well, a call center must have an excellent telephone system and multiple telephone numbers with headsets; we need trained employees, and product information readily available to answer difficult questions. All of these will pass the "Is it critical?" question, with the possible exception of training. Training may be necessary, but it's also possible that the organization's employees are already experienced in call center operations. If not, then training will become an objective. Experienced supervisors will also be a goal or objective. Measuring call center performance will also be essential; we'll talk about how to do that in later chapters.

Interviewing

As we discussed in Chapter 3, interviewing key people (internal management or process individuals or customers) can produce excellent information and allow you to gain buy-in for your stated objectives.[5] The purpose of these interviews is to help identify what items are critical to achieving the improvement initiative you're about to launch. A lot goes into conducting an effective interview, but I'll generalize here and attempt to cover the most salient points. There are a few principles that are "musts" in conducting efficient and effective interviews:

- Questioner should be very knowledgeable of the CSFs, should be relaxed, and have questions already prepared. He or she can leapfrog to other related items if the opportunity presents itself and appears to be a beneficial pursuit. Conduct the interview in an office, conference room, or somewhere where it is quiet. Take notes, summarize, and analyze after the interview.

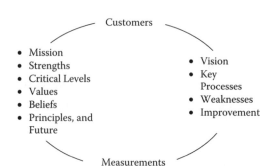

Figure 4.4 Subject coverage areas for interview questions.

■ Interviewee should be relaxed, answer questions accurately, and vision the future when opportunities arise.

■ In developing the questions, the analyst can use brainstorming or the modified nominal group technique. Form a team and use one of these techniques to generate the questions, then prioritize, consolidate, add, and delete until a focused, adequate series of questions are formulated. See Figure 4.4 for the possible subject areas for the questions.

■ Tailor your interview to who is being interviewed. The proper strategy will often depend on the position held, their personality, organizational culture, financial position, knowledge of the subject area, and other factors.

■ Taking notes is situational. Taking notes takes more time and slows the interview. Also, it is imperative in many situations that the information written is kept confidential. If notes are not taken, the analyst should summarize the interview quickly after it is over, to list the pertinent information obtained. Don't give in to the temptation to conduct an online or written survey for anonymity's sake. Since the individuals you are interviewing will have different perspectives and experience, a survey may not uncover the nuances that an interview may.

The questions asked might include:

■ What is the mission of your organization?
■ What functions, products, or services do you perform or produce now? Plans for new ones in the future?
■ How many employees? Full-time? Part-time? Contractors?
■ Who are your customers?
■ What are their requirements?
■ How are you meeting these requirements? How do you know?

- Does your organization have a vision?
- How do you relate to the vision or impact it?
- What performance improvement initiatives are you implementing now? Planned for the future? (Determine whether this is a management-driven initiative or a technical-driven one, such as construction.)
- What things do you envision as important to successfully achieving this effort?
- What are your organization's measures and which ones are you trying to improve? For the latter, what is the current status and what do you wish to accomplish (your target)?
- What are your actions or plans to achieve these improvements?
- What are the barriers you foresee in accomplishing these activities/actions?
- What factors do you consider important to your organization's success? For example, top management commitment, employee involvement, etc.? (Let the interviewee review the traditional list to see if any of these CSFs are important to his or her objective.)
- Are there any critical levels of production, performance, etc., important to your organization?
- What are your key processes?
- Are they stable (in statistical control)?
- Have you had any audits, customer complaints, etc., that highlight problem areas in performance or in any of your organization's operations?
- If you could improve one thing now in your organization, what would it be?
- How do you measure whether you are successful?
- What do you envision in the future that could harm your organization? Threats, weaknesses, events, etc.?
- What opportunities do you foresee in the future?
- What do you consider your organization's strengths?
- How would you define critical success factors as they might affect your organization?
- If you think of any additional information, would you please give me a call?

Before you conduct the interview, it can be helpful to review your organization's mission, vision, strategic goals and objectives, action plans, and performance measures. This preinterview preparation often can help identify possible CSFs. To generate ideas from the group on possible CSFs, use brainstorming (see Appendix B) or the modified nominal group technique (see Appendix C).

Traditional List

In my experience, forty-two CSFs are commonly used during management improvement initiatives. Normally, five to seven are identified and used for each improvement effort or initiative. By keeping your CSFs to a manageable number—neither too many nor too few—you can ensure a fairly broad reach while avoiding the scatter approach, or simply implementing every CSF you can think of and seeing what sticks.

Each CSF can be further broken down into several subfactors that can be helpful in selecting the correct ones for your objective. By identifying the subfactors, you'll be better equipped to measure the implementation progress of the CSF. The traditional list (TL) is included as Appendix D. A few examples from the TL are:

1. Accountability
   - Responsible for actions taken, both performance and quality
   - Understands what is expected from management and the team charter or job description and strives to achieve
   - Individual is competent in the tasks, job, process, program, etc.; if not, training, experience, and education should be provided
2. Best practices
   - Employees' input as to best practices they have used or observed
   - Benchmarking—both internal and external
   - Internet research for best methods
   - Best practices recorded and placed in work or process instructions
3. Client relationship
   - Gets along well with clients
   - Understands their needs
   - Delivery meets exceptional performance requirement and clients agree
   - Builds trust
   - When clients need a product or service, they think of you
4. Coaching/facilitating
   - Helping individuals, people, teams, or groups learn a new skill or tool, or follow a process or procedure
   - Passing on best practices or skills
   - Keeping team on track
   - Setting agendas that drive improvement
   - Solving problems
   - Generating issues
   - Learning new tools or techniques

5. Communication
  - Internal communications
  - External communications plan
  - Written news on subject
  - Common language on subject material
  - Speeches on subject
  - Communicating why we are doing this
  - Communicating expectations
  - Providing pertinent facts, including successes and reasons for failure
6. Constancy of purpose
  - Obtaining a focus
  - Staying on course until objectives or visions are achieved
  - From start of an initiative, staying on path or road map to conclusion
7. Continual improvement
  - Uses PDCA (plan-do-check-act) philosophy and keeps turning the wheel (PDCA:PDCA) for continuous improvement
  - Performs management reviews
  - Leadership dedicated, knowledgeable, and challenging
  - Everyone seeks ways to improve operations and processes
8. Cost system
  - Cost accumulation by activity/product/service
  - Cost analysis
  - Cost information—timely, accurate, complete, and accessible; reports can be generated
  - Cost-effective system that meets cost data and analysis needs

For some management initiatives, several of the traditional CSFs listed above will be critical.[6] For example, top management commitment/executive engagement is critical to ISO 9000 (Processes), ISO 14001 (Environmental Management System), Six Sigma (a quality and process improvement initiative that produces products that have only 3.2 errors, defaults, or failures in every million produced), strategic planning, and Lean office/manufacturing (a process improvement technique that eliminates waste in a process). Management/executive reviews are also critical to each. Table 4.1 shows how CSFs are common to the success of various improvement initiatives.

Remember, the key question is: "Is this factor *critical* to the success of the improvement initiative (ISO 9000, ISO 14001, Six Sigma, etc.)?" If the answer is yes, then it is a CSF. As shown above, there are several common CSFs and a few pertinent to only one or two initiatives but not to the others.

Table 4.1 CSFs Common to the Success of Various Improvement Initiatives

Strategic Planning	ISO 9000	ISO 14001	Six Sigma	Lean
1. Top management commitment	Same	Same	Same	Same
2. Cross-functional management			Training	Training
3. Communications	Same	Same	Same	Same
4. Employee involvement	Same	Same		Same
5. Resources allocated	Same	Same	Same	
6. Objectives and targets		Same	Same	Same
7. Measurement			Same	Same
8. Problem-solving process			Same	Same
9. Executive/management reviews	Same	Same	Same	Same
10. Recognition/rewards		Same		

Of course, these CSFs can vary from organization to organization due to different products and services, location, and where in the implementation process they were identified. But note that you don't necessarily have to reinvent the wheel: considering traditional CSFs first can save you time in the identification process.

Writing the CSFs

Written CSFs can be short, medium, or long in length. Federal, state, city, and military organizations often use the long format or at least the medium one. However, writing short CSFs makes for easier communication and remembrance. As stated in Chapter 3, the goal length for CSFs should be ten words or less. Writing CSF subfactors (as done in the traditional list) can add depth and understanding to your CSF statements, and assist in measuring your CSFs.

Let's look at Oklahoma State University's CSF statements (OSU-Oklahoma City Strategic Plan <http://system.okstate.edu/planning/plans/viewplans_okc.php>). Oklahoma State uses CSFs in their strategic planning to help ensure that their goals, objectives, and strategies are achieved. Their CSFs are measurable: "Increase program graduates to 750. Increase student retention rate to 70% (fall to spring)." These are great, provided that they are truly critical to the success of the objective and not just best practices or strategies. What's the distinction? A best practice or strategy may or may not help you achieve your objective. Conversely, a CSF achieved *will* enable you to achieve your objective.

Step 5: Measure CSF Implementation Progress

The selected CSFs should show improved performance as the initiative's performance increases. For example, CSFs for an environmental measurement system (EMS), such as top management commitment and communications, should increase as the degree of the EMS implementation increases (see Chapter 7 for an example of CSFs for EMS implementation).

In this and following chapters, I'll demonstrate seven methods of measuring CSF progress, and let you know when to use each. Select the technique most useful or appropriate to your situation. Remember, what gets measured, gets done.

The seven methods best suited for measuring CSF implementation follow.

Method 1: Stages—Start to Finish Implementation Method

Before you begin to implement an initiative, determine the stages each CSF will go through, from start to completion. Assign a 1 to the start condition and a 5 to the stage or condition that reflects completion or total implementation. Let's say that you're tracking and measuring each CSF on a monthly basis. Each month, each CSF has the potential to receive a score of 1 (beginning implementation) to 5 (total implementation). The highest possible score is your number of CSFs times 5. (For example, if you're implementing and tracking seven CSFs, your highest possible score will be 35, if all CSFs are totally implemented [7 CSFs × highest possible score of 5 = 35].) Each implementation team member will score the CSFs separately. To determine the percentage of the CSFs that have been implemented, the implementation team needs to add all scores for each CSF, divided by the total members of the team, and multiplied by 100 (Table 4.2).

Team Member	CSF 1	CSF 2	CSF 3	CSF 4	CSF 5	CSF 6	CSF 7	Total Score
John	3	2	4	3	2	3	1	18
Norman	2	3	3	3	3	2	2	18
Carol	3	3	3	3	2	2	3	19
Bill	2	2	3	2	3	3	2	17
Jack	3	3	3	2	3	2	3	19
Score	13	13	16	13	13	12	11	91

Table 4.2   Percentage of CSFs Implemented

As you can see in Table 4.2, the total score for this particular example is 91. There were five team members voting. Therefore, for this month the total score to graph is 18.2. This is the average of the total scores (91/5 = 18.2). The degree of implementation is determined by dividing 18.2 by the highest possible score of 35 (7 CSFs × 5). If all team members gave each CSF the highest possible score, the total would be 175; 175/5 (team members) = 35—the highest score an individual can vote. So, by dividing our score of 18.2 by 35, we can see that the CSFs have been 52% implemented. We have a lot of implementation left to attend to.

The CSF with the highest degree of implementation is CSF 3. The CSF with the lowest degree of implementation is CSF 7. This type of tracking system enables the team to take immediate action when one or more CSFs are lagging behind in implementation. In this instance, it would be appropriate for the team to plan on how they could increase CSFs 6 and 7. After implementing the plan, the team can continue to track the CSFs on a monthly or quarterly basis to determine whether their improvements have had the desired impact.

What happens next depends on the team members' perception of the degree of implementation of each CSF (see Chapter 5 for an example of how this technique might play out during ISO 14001 EMS implementation).

Briefly, however, let's take a look at a top management commitment CSF. What does a 1 look like, when management is not involved in supporting the initiative? What would a 5 look like, with management fully engaged? Next, determine what increasing commitment, from 2 to 4, would look like:

1. Not involved or at least involvement is not noticeable or visible to employees
2. Approved the program or effort, does talk the talk sometimes

3. Participates in some meetings, also gives verbal support
4. Involved, shows commitment, provides support and resources
5. Very committed, walks the talk, and asks for updates; chairs management reviews; provides leadership

Method 2: Critical Success Levels

The critical success level (CSL) technique can be used when there is a critical level that must be reached for the organization to be successful. For example, just as an individual needs a specific amount of money to meet his or her monthly expenses, a production system needs to produce a specific number of products daily to meet customers' demand. Therefore, to use the CSL technique, you must first determine the levels of production or service that are absolutely critical to success. Use these levels (number of sales per month, number of parts produced per week, operating at 3 Sigma or higher quality levels, specifications levels, etc.) to measure your actual performance vs. the CSLs. Your strategy CSFs should help you set your CSLs. Be sure to measure your actual vs. CSL levels monthly, or more frequently, to determine how well you are performing. If you're not performing up to par, it's time to take corrective action.

For example, a car dealership needs to make sales greater than $300,000 a quarter to break even. That is their CSL. In February, they sold $99,000 worth of cars; in March, they sold $150,000; and in April, they sold only $75,000. How did they do? They sold $324,000 ($99,000 + $150,000 + $75,000) during the quarter. This compares favorably with the dealership's CSL of $300,000, as they not only broke even but actually made a small profit. (See Chapter 8 for an additional example of this measurement technique.)

Method 3: SMART Objectives and Targets

This technique consists of establishing objectives and targets and then measuring their performance. Again, SMART stands for:

- Specific
- Measurable
- Actionable
- Relevant and realistic
- Time framed

Examples are:

■ Decrease rework by 20% during the year 2007
■ Enhance our image so customers rate us as high performers (5 or higher) on our annual customer satisfaction survey
■ Achieve world-class status by winning the Deming prize for quality by 2010
■ Increase our workforce productivity by 10% by the end of 2008
■ Increase our customer base from 6 million to 10 million by the end of 2008

Your CSFs are the items that are critical to making your SMART objectives happen.

Method 4: Traditional Industry Measures

Many companies use traditional measures as a target, for example, that 90% of customer inquiries are answered within one hour, or that 95% of customers are retained per year, or telephone calls are answered in three rings or less. These traditional industry CSFs are often very useful. Identifying the CSF and an appropriate measure for determining its degree of implementation are key steps in improving performance of any improvement initiative.

Method 5: "Traffic Light" Measures

We often think of metrics simply as data graphed on a chart with a target. Almost all organizations conduct periodic comparisons of their present performance or the trend of several months' performance to the desired target. When your company's actual performance doesn't match its target performance, you need to take action to correct the situation. This is the hard data approach, and is excellent if the data are available. However, a soft measure can be very useful even when the data are not available. An excellent soft measure is use of the traffic light approach. See Figure 4.5 for the stoplight descriptions.

Green	Yellow	Red
Description of good performance	Description of poor performance	Description of bad performance

Figure 4.5 Stoplight measure descriptions.

Green	Yellow	Red
1. Environmental policy developed and communicated	1. Environmental policy developed and communicated	1. Environmental policy established but not clear
2. Environmental aspects identified, ranked and significant aspects determined	2. Environmental aspects identified, ranked and significant aspects determined	2. Some aspects established
3. Environmental impacts determined	3. Environmental impacts determined	3. Impacts partially identified
4. Legal and other requirements identified	4. No legal and other requirements identified	4. No legal requirements identified
5. Objectives and targets established	5. Objectives and targets established	5. Some objectives being pursued
6. Environmental Management Programs (EMPs) developed	6. Some actions identified	6. No actions identified for implementation
7. All employees given EMS awareness training	7. All employees given EMS awareness training	7. No employee trained

Figure 4.6   Planning an ISO 14001 environmental management system (EMS).

Red equals poor or unsatisfactory performance, yellow indicates a need for improvement, and green is on target. If you're above target, best in class, or world class, you can use blue as your stoplight measure—you're in a place where there's no traffic light, no traffic, and blue skies.

For example, the area being measured, environmental performance, includes indicators of what constitutes a red, yellow, or green performance. The scorer reads the criteria in each and selects which area best represents the organization's current phase of implementation (Figure 4.6). The organization is then assigned that particular color for the month being scored.

This technique drives action. No one wants to be in the red. If they are, they will start immediately identifying what they need to do to become at least a yellow.

	Very Good	Good	Average	Some-times	Hardly At All	Don't Know
1. Our leadership walks the talk.	5	4	3	2	1	0
2. Our leaders communicate the vision.	5	4	3	2	1	0
3. Leaders in our organization are involved and support our activities.	5	4	3	2	1	0
4. Our leaders both recognize and reward employees' performance.	5	4	3	2	1	0

Figure 4.7 Leadership survey.

Method 6: Surveys

Method 6 is used when you do not have any quantitative data (data you can count, such as kilowatts, dollar sales, or yield). Using surveys, you can gather, calculate, and graph data on an almost limitless number of topics. Although it is a soft measure, it looks like a hard measure and often is treated as such. Consider the following example, in which an organization wrote and administered a survey containing the key characteristics of leadership, and then tabulated and communicated the results (Figure 4.7).

Survey results were tabulated in the first quarter (Figure 4.8). The survey was then administered again in the second quarter for the fifty people in the area of focus (Figure 4.9).

From the above survey, we can see that our leaders can improve in all areas, but supporting our employees, including recognizing and rewarding their performance, is the area that needs their focus the most.

In this instance, the leadership of the organization reviewed the first-quarter results and committed to making improvements. They set up a cross-functional recognition and award team to review recommendations for awards. The most deserving were selected and, depending on the significance of their achievement, awards were presented at either employee/management meetings or in person by one of the top managers. The vision was posted in places easy to read by most people. Management discussed it at every opportunity—in town hall meetings, staff meetings, recognition meetings, strategic planning meetings, department meetings, etc.

	Questions	5	4	3	2	1	
First Quarter	1.	10	20	5	4	11	Number of votes
	2.	21	7	19	0	3	
Results	3.	2	2	13	18	15	
	4.	8	7	15	10	10	

1. Do the leaders walk the talk?   Yes_____   No_____
2. Is the vision communicated well?   Yes_____   No_____
3. Are the leaders involved and supportive?   Yes_____   No_____
4. Do the leaders recognize and reward employees?   Yes_____   No_____

What does the data say?

Question 1 $10 \times 5 + 20 \times 4 + 5 \times 3 + 4 \times 2 + 11 \times 1$

$50 + 80 + 15 + 8 + 11 = \dfrac{164}{50} = 3.28$

Between average and good.

Question 2 $21 \times 5 + 7 \times 4 + 19 \times 3 + 0 \times 2 + 3 \times 1$

$105 + 25 + 57 + 0 + 3 = \dfrac{193}{50} = 3.86$

Close to being good.

Question 3 $2 \times 5 + 2 \times 4 + 13 \times 3 + 18 \times 2 + 15 \times 1$

$10 + 8 + 39 + 36 + 15 = \dfrac{108}{50} = 2.16$ is close to sometimes.

Question 4 $8 \times 5 + 7 \times 4 + 15 \times 3 + 10 \times 2 + 10 \times 1$

$40 + 28 + 45 + 20 + 10 = \dfrac{143}{50} = 2.86$ close to average.

Questions	Answers
• Our leadership walks the talk	Between average and good
• Our leaders communicate the vision	Good
• Leaders in our organization are involved and support our activities	Sometimes
• Our leaders recognize and reward employees' performance	Average

Figure 4.8   First-quarter results.

	Questions	5	4	3	2	1	
Second Quarter	1.	32	7	5	4	2	50 people took the survey
	2.	40	4	2	1	3	
Results	3.	20	10	15	3	2	
	4.	28	15	5	2	0	

Figure 4.9   Second-quarter results.

Results data:

Question 1 $32 \times 5 + 7 \times 4 + 5 \times 3 + 4 \times 2 + 2 \times 1$

$160 + 28 + 15 + 8 + 2 = \dfrac{213}{50} = 4.26$

is between good and very good

$4.26 - 3.28 = .98$ $\dfrac{.98}{3.28} \times 100 = 29.9\%$ increase
Good improvement.

Question 2 $40 \times 5 + 4 \times 4 + 2 \times 3 + 1 \times 2 + 3 \times 1$

$200 + 16 + 6 + 2 + 3 = \dfrac{227}{50} = 4.54$

4.54 is between good and very good

$4.54 - 3.86 = .68$ $\dfrac{.68}{3.86} \times 100 = 17.6\%$ improvement over last survey

Good improvement.

Question 3 $20 \times 5 + 10 \times 4 + 15 \times 3 + 3 \times 2 + 2 \times 1$

$100 + 40 + 45 + 6 + 2 = \dfrac{193}{50} = 3.86$

3.86 is between average and good – close to good

$3.86 - 2.16 = .70$ $\dfrac{.70}{2.16} \times 100 = 32.4\%$
Definite improvement. Significant.

Question 4 $28 \times 5 + 15 \times 4 + 5 \times 3 + 2 \times 2 + 0 \times 1$

$140 + 60 + 15 + 4 + 0 = \dfrac{219}{50} = 4.38$

4.38 is between good and very good

$4.38 - 2.86 = 1.52$ $\dfrac{1.52}{2.86} \times 100 = 53.1\%$ increase
A major increase.

The leadership survey was administered again in the next quarter (Figure 4.9). Even though it had only been a short time since the company recognition and award team was formed, top management hoped that the survey would show significant improvement. The survey was administered in the second quarter for the same fifty people in the area of focus. So what were the results?

The leadership countermeasures are working, and excellent progress is being made.

Method 7: Striving for Coverage—The "Scatter Approach"

Often the measure(s) of identified CSFs' implementation progress can be accomplished by what I call the scatter approach. In this approach, you think of everything that you can that seems to have some impact on the CSF when the trend goes a certain direction. Next, you measure all of the data that are readily available and hope that the CSF is covered.

Let's say that we have an organization that produces circuit boards for computers. They must have a quality workforce to compete in the industry, and they must produce quality products. The measures they selected are:

1. Employees' satisfaction with the training
2. The number of hours each employee receives in training each year
3. The number of personnel qualified at skill levels X and Y (or percent of total employees that are at skill levels X and Y)

The above measures are three good ones, but was the training the right training? Did productivity or quality of the output increase? Are production targets being achieved? How pleased are the process owners? It may be costly to periodically gather and graph data that may not add any value. Using criteria that are reproducible, cost-effective, accurate, and send the right message to select individual measures/indicators can help you to select the best measure(s) and ensure good coverage.

Selecting the Right Indicator

Indicators or measures are derived from your processes or objectives.[7] Processes include inputs, the process itself, the output (a product, service, or information), and outcomes. Measures can come from each of these areas. From inputs come supplier measures. The process itself has numerous measures that gauge progress and quality at various activities in the process. The outputs show volume and quality measures. Outcomes include customer satisfaction and stakeholder's satisfaction. Objectives automatically include measures when they are made SMART. The indicator(s) selected should be:

- Measurable
- Reproducible/auditable
- Timely
- Cost-effective
- Send the right message*

If collecting indicator data, then it may or may not be feasible to use it. The value achieved must be higher than the cost to produce it. For example, to collect data from all work processes may cost hundreds of thousands of dollars. Perhaps checking only the key processes will suffice. When in doubt, use the costs-benefits technique, covered in most economics books. If someone else graphed the indicator, the same results should occur (reproducible/audible). Measures must be timely (current) or they will not drive appropriate action.

Indicators must send the right message. For example, one organization selected the number of internal audit findings as a key indicator. It felt that if the number of findings went down, it would be doing a better job and the annual external audit would be an improvement over the last one.

On the surface, this logic sounds good. However, the reason for the internal audit is to determine what is wrong and fix it prior to the external audit. The results of the external audit are extremely important to the organization's performance recognition by stakeholders, including customers. Therefore, a management decrease of audit findings on internal audit findings would lessen the audit's effectiveness. When an outside auditor comes in, he or she may find violations that should have been highlighted by the internal auditors but weren't because the internal auditors were trying to make management happy.

Let's look at another example. This particular company's goal is to reduce the amount of hazardous materials shipped by 10% this year. Employees try to give management what they want. If management wants the amount of hazardous materials shipped to be 10% less than it was last year, it will be done. However, if no countermeasures or intended solutions (including actions and resources) are employed, the objective will most probably be

---

* Reprinted with permission of American Society for Quality (ASQ).

met by manipulation. Employees will ship them next year, holding on to them when they should not. The result? Hazardous materials that should have been shipped remain in the workplace for an extended time.

Selecting the right indicator can sometimes be tricky. For years, baseball teams thought a hitter's batting average (number of hits divided by total number of times at bat) was a key measure of the person's value to the team and the best measure of his or her productivity at bat. But then the Oakland Athletics started using on-base percentage, defined as hits plus walks plus hit by pitches, divided by number of times at the plate. This proved to be a better measure of productivity in hitting. The more times on base, the better the chance to score. The number of runs determines the winner.[8]

All CSFs Are Not Created Equal

Most of the time, CSFs are treated as if each is equally important. In reality, that seldom occurs. For example, in implementing a management program or initiative such as Lean or Six Sigma, top management commitment or support will probably be more important than any other CSF selected. Without top management commitment, the initiative will fail. Employees will lose motivation, necessary resources will not be provided, and no recognition for efforts accomplished will be extended by management. The improvement initiative will either stop quickly or fizzle out over time, with effort decreasing as time goes by.

Let's say top management commitment, communications, recognition, objectives, and planning were selected as our CSFs. Let's rank them from 1 to 5. The results are:

1 Top management commitment
2 Planning
3 Objectives
4 Communications
5 Recognition

Now to be useful, we need to assign some weight as to how they ranked. Let's say for example we assign a score of 10 for rank 1, 7 for rank 2, 5 for rank 3, 3 for rank 4, and 1 for rank 5.

Figure 4.10 shows us the weights.

When the team determines the progress of each CSF's implementation, the score result is multiplied by the weights. They are then summed to get

Top management commitment	10
Planning	7
Objectives	5
Communications	3
Recognition	1

Figure 4.10   Weights.

one figure for the month. Conversely, instead of being ranked, each CSF can be given a weight from 1 to 10, which will accomplish the same function of assigning importance.

If you'd prefer, instead of using a scale of 10, you can use 100 as your measure and think of the weights as percentages. The question then is: "What percent should each CSF have of the total percent (100%)?"

Although weights can be assigned in several ways, using the 1 to 5 scale is an excellent method for assigning weights to a CSF. The weights are:

Not Very Important		*Important*	*Very Important*	*Extremely Important*
1	2	3	4	5

An example of this is:

CSF	*Weights*
Top Management	5
Planning	4
Objectives	4
Communications	3
Recognition	2

The 1 to 5 scale is useful in assessing the progress of what a CSF has achieved during the initiative's implementation.

Graph the CSF's Performance

It is important to graph each CSF to highlight both good performance and any areas needing corrective action. Individual graphs can provide you with a picture that immediately tells how you are doing. Normally a bar or column chart or a line graph is appropriate for graphing a CSF's performance. Alternatively, you can use a spider diagram to show all CSFs on one chart. Develop a data collection plan for each CSF, collect the data, post graphs, and discuss with the team to ensure that the right graph was selected.

Let's take a look at this in practice.

CSF	(A) Implementation Progress	(B) Weight	(A x B) Total Score
Top management commitment	3	5	15
Planning	4	4	16
Objectives	4	4	16
Communication	2	3	6
Recognition	1	2	2

Fifty-five is the total score. It represents 61% of the possible score (the highest possible score for each CSF is $5 \times 5 + 4 \times 5 + 4 \times 5 + 3 \times 5 + 2 \times 5 = 90$ total possible points).

$$\text{Percentage} = \frac{55}{90} \times 100 = 61\%$$

The score or percentage obtained can be plotted monthly to show progress (Figure 4.11), the trend, and highlight a problem if the trend is not going up monthly or at least staying at the same level. Remember, the weights stay the same, month by month, but the scores come from assigning implementation levels for each CSF, from 1 to 5. These will change. They should become higher as time goes by and as the CSFs are more completely implemented.

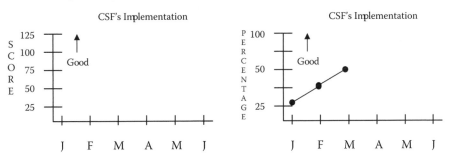

Figure 4.11 CSF graphs.

Step 6: Monitor and Take Action

Once an improvement initiative has been completed, don't abandon it by moving on to something else and not keeping track. Things can go wrong, situations can develop, unforeseen circumstances can occur. I can't overemphasize the importance of the check and act steps on the Deming wheel. During the sixth step, you'll monitor your CSFs and take action if any CSF's performance is subpar. You'll need to develop and implement an action plan that encompasses the who, what, why, when, where, and how. Check your implementation progress and take corrective action if needed.

Here's an example:

Problem: Top management not committed (received a score of 3)

Plan: Team schedules meeting that involves top management (for example, an orientation meeting). Identify benefits of what they are doing, determine present situation, and show how management can help. Ask and gain their support. You cannot expect top management to always jump on board right away on all new initiatives. It helps if the idea for doing the improvement was theirs. If not, then they should be engaged by the project or objective leader and his or her team to get them on board and involved. Have some recommendations available that they can easily do and show support for the initiative.

Problem: Resources not made available.

Plan: Team identifies what is needed (low cost but effective), writes justification, shows cost vs. benefits, and submits to appropriate office for approval. Follow up periodically. If called, be ready to present or defend the recommendation for resources, including dollars.

Six-Step Process Example: Implementing a Productivity Program

Let's take a simple improvement initiative and use the six steps outlined above. These steps are:

1. Define the goals and objectives of the initiative.
2. Identify the CSFs.
3. Select the appropriate CSFs.
4. Determine subfactors for each selected CSF.

5. Measure CSFs' implementation progress.
6. Monitor and take action.

Step 1: Define the Goals and Objectives of the Initiative

Step 1 will help us formalize our goals and objectives. Goals are brief and long range. They represent what you want to accomplish in three to ten years. Some examples are:

- Improve quality
- Enhance our image
- Achieve world-class status
- Improve workforce productivity (productivity improvement selected—a goal for the problem selected)
- Satisfy stakeholders
- Increase our company base
- Be a process-based company
- Be known as a reliable, professional company

Objectives are specific, short term, and SMART. For this initiative, our objective might be to improve productivity of the XLY workforce by 10% by the end of calendar year 2012.

Although we've covered how to identify CSFs in this and prior chapters, let's look at this process again, in relation to improving productivity at an organization.

Step 2: Identify the CSFs

Generate a list of possible CSFs that may help to achieve the above objective. This can be done by a team who is either involved in establishing the objectives or tasked to identify strategies and projects to accomplish them. For small organizations or limited objectives, one or two individuals may generate the list. Brainstorming, green lighting, or the modified nominal group technique are good ways to generate possible CSFs.

Green lighting occurs in brainstorming after the group has put up possible CSFs in sequenced order and the brainstorming process has slowed down. It is allowed then for anyone to talk (out of turn) if they have an idea. A list may look like this:

1. Top management commitment
2. Resources provided
3. Measurement
4. Communication
5. Employee involvement
6. Objectives and targets
7. Training
8. Best practices
9. Time to accomplish project
10. Sincerity
11. Continuous improvement

Now we have a possible list of CSFs to use. To select the critical ones, go to step 3.

Step 3: Select the Appropriate CSFs

For the list of possible CSFs, ask the question: "Is this CSF critical to achieving the objective?" In other words, would productivity improve? Answer yes or no (Figure 4.12). Remember, some of these can be either a KRA or CSF, depending on their purpose. In this case, their purpose makes all of them CSFs.

Objective: Implement a Productivity Program by December 31, 2007					
1. Top management commitment	Critical	×	Yes		No
2. Resources provided		×	Yes		No
3. Measurement		×	Yes		No
4. Communications		×	Yes		No
5. Employee involvement		×	Yes		No
6. Objectives and targets		×	Yes		No
7. Training		×	Yes		No
8. Best practices		×	Yes		No
9. Time to accomplish project			Yes	×	No
10. Sincerity			Yes	×	No
11. Continuous improvement			Yes	×	No

Figure 4.12   Determining criticality.

Next, take the CSFs for which an X indicates yes; they are critical to achieving the objective. Now, see if any that received a yes are close in meaning to another. If so, combine those two. If you have more than eight, discuss and reduce the list to only the essential critical factors.

Step 4: Determine Subfactors for Each Selected CSF

This step helps the team to understand the CSF and to develop measures to track its implementation progress. For each CSF, what are the factors that pertain to it or its composition? See Figure 4.13.

1. Resources provided
   - Sufficient to accomplish the project(s) or achieve the objectives
   - Timely and useful
   - Managed (project management) and efficiently utilized
2. Measurement
   - Actionable performance indicators (meaningful, provide adequate coverage, cost-effective, identified and graphed)
   - Data collection plan for each indicator
   - Targets or standards established
   - Indicators kept current and visible
   - Readily accessible to people needing the information
3. Communication
   - Internal communications
   - External communication plan
   - Written news on subject
   - Common language on subject material
   - Speeches on subject
   - Communicating why we are doing this
   - Expectations are presented
   - Providing pertinent facts, including successes and reasons for failure

Figure 4.13   CSF subfactors.

4. Employee involvement
   - Understands objectives, vision, process, etc., and is involved in the improvement or performance
   - Trained or educated in what needs to be done
   - Possesses sufficient experience—competent in the tasks/activities involved
5. Objectives and targets
   - Objectives are established
   - Made SMART (specific, measurable, actionable, relevant, and time framed)
   - Realistic, but stretch targets, limits, or standards are established, in which goals are reasonable but not necessarily easily achieved
   - Actions identified, that if done, will achieve the objective(s)
   - Linked to objectives, goals, key result areas, or vision
   - A champion or a responsible person assigned to each objective
   - Action plans developed to achieve the objective
6. Training
   - Specific: What is needed to accomplish a task, process, or solve a problem
   - The tools or techniques needed to accomplish the objectives, job, task, process, action plan, etc., or to solve a problem
   - Training for team leaders, facilitators, team members; process improvement tools, the reengineering process, strategic planning, Lean manufacturing, Six Sigma, black belt, green belt, yellow belt, teamwork, statistics, group dynamics, and measurement are examples for improvement training (training will vary depending on need); generally, starts with awareness training (broad overview) and then gets to specifics (how to accomplish specific tasks or use a tool or technique)
7. Best practices
   - Employees' input as to best practices
   - Benchmarking—both internal and external
   - Internet research for best methods
   - Best practices recorded and placed in work or process instructions

Step 5: Measure CSFs' Implementation Progress

Once the subfactors are identified, your team is ready to measure the CSFs' implementation progress of the productivity program. Determine for each

CSF what the start looks like (assign it a 1) at the beginning and what the end looks like (assign it a 5) when it has been fully achieved. For example, top management commitment:

Score	Description of Commitment
1	Not involved
2	Provides verbal support and communicates benefits
3	Provides resources, motivates team, and is involved
4	Actively supports, provides resources, and is there when team needs them
5	A leader, supporter; provides ideas, rewards and recognizes efforts, and helps "make it happen"

Do this type of quantification for each selected CSF. Every month, your team will vote on where the CSF has progressed. At the beginning, they would select a score of 1. Over time, progress would lead to selecting higher scores. The votes are added up and divided by the number of team members voting. All of the CSFs scores are added up and plotted on a line graph.

Although we've used measurement method 1 here, other measurement techniques could also have been selected.[9] The critical level (CL) measurement technique could apply here also. Productivity would be the normal CL. However, direct work from work sampling or rework would be two other possibilities for a productivity improvement program measure of success. Establishing objectives and then making them SMART can provide another performance measure. Even the stoplight approach would be useful, by first identifying what constitutes a poor productivity program, a program needing improvement, and a productive program. Your team can then determine where you land on that scale and plan how to get to a higher level of improvement.

Step 6: Monitor and Take Action

When you're monitoring your CSFs, as long as improvements are being made, there's no need to take action. If a problem appears, then corrective action is needed. First, you need to determine the root causes of the problem. The best tool for discovering potential root causes is the fishbone diagram, sometimes called a cause-and-effect diagram (Figure 4.14). Once the root cause has been identified, develop countermeasures to get the CSFs moving. Look at the next two levels in the CSF possible scores. This will give your team ideas on what

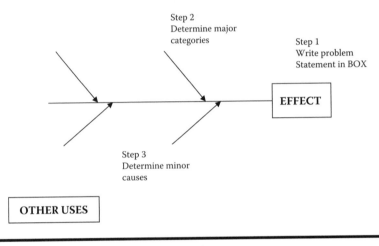

PURPOSE

Identification of potential root causes so that countermeasures can be applied.

WHAT IS IT?

Lines and words designed to represent a meaningful relationship between an effect (problem) and its causes.
Ishikawa Diagram or Fishbone are two other common names.

Step 2
Determine major
categories

Step 1
Write problem
Statement in BOX

EFFECT

Step 3
Determine minor
causes

OTHER USES

Figure 4.14 Fishbone, or cause-and-effect, diagram.

needs to be done next. For example, to achieve a score of 2 to 3, what must happen? Plan for this to happen and initiate action to ensure that it will.

A fishbone diagram can help a group or team understand a problem and can show gaps in existing knowledge. Once the possible root causes are identified, their symptoms are verified by using data analysis or team observations. For each root cause, you'll need to develop and implement a countermeasure or solution. This technique should be utilized every time a major problem or barrier occurs. See Mears[10] for more detailed information.

Implementing CSFs Organization-wide

Next, let's discuss the process for implementing CSFs organization-wide.

First, form a top management steering group, executive board, budget and financial group, or executive strategic planning team to decide the benefits, and how to implement, promote, and communicate the effort. Their duties are:

- Make the decision to go for it.
- Develop a policy on governing the uses of CSFs in the organization, such as for all strategic planning teams, business planning, functional planning, systems implementation and improvements initiatives such as ISO 9000 or 14001, Six Sigma, and Lean office or manufacturing.
- Provide resources for training and determine the targeted participants (department heads, cross-functional team members, natural working groups, managers, and supervisors).
- Communicate the objectives of the CSF program to all employees.
- Perform management reviews.
- Recognize and reward successes. Provide specific awards that are appropriate to the achievement, given in a timely fashion, and meaningful to the recipient.

CSFs can be used effectively by department heads, supervisors, project managers, and individuals to achieve success in their initiatives without top management guidance and support. However, to make it an organization-wide program, top management buy-in and support is a critical success factor.

Once management is on board, you'll need to train the participants to use CSFs for improvement initiatives. This can be done through the train-the-trainer method or through training targeted groups as to when they start the CSF use program. Training should include:

- What is a CSF?
- How are they identified?
- CSF methods
- CSF achievement model
- Measures of success
- Six methods of CSF measurement
- Tying CSFs to organizational improvements
- Exercises in identifying and measuring CSF implementation progress

After the training, require each manager to develop his or her CSFs for his or her goals and objectives. Have him or her present these during budget submittals or budget reviews.

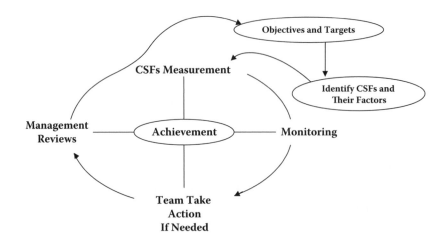

Figure 4.15   The achievement cycle.

Remember, CSFs can be used at any level of an organization, from the top down. The key here is that organizational CSFs be developed for the *organizational element* that the improvement initiative is targeting. This can be for an organization-wide initiative, such as strategic planning, or for improving a process in one or two departments, assuming that the process includes activities in both of these departments.

For all chartered teams (strategic planning, corporate cross-functional teams, ISO 9000 process or ISO 14001 EMS teams, Six Sigma teams, reengineering teams, and Lean teams), have them identify the CSFs that will make their pursuits and efforts successful. Require them to use the CSF achievement model. Encourage all teams and department managers to identify CSFs when appropriate to help them achieve their goals and objectives. Identify success stories and communicate them in presentations, staff meetings, and town meetings, mainly to build up interest and desire to use CSFs.

The six-step method will enable any organization to effectively implement a CSF program. If the organization does not implement a CSF program, any department or individual can still use CSFs to drive his or her initiatives simply by using the above CSF achievement method. The achievement cycle in Figure 4.15 shows the activities necessary for full implementation, success, and continual improvement.

The real test of CSFs is the following: if they are achieved, then is the program, initiative, or objective being implemented also simultaneously achieved?

Figure 4.15 shows what we have known all along: what gets measured, gets improved. This is the cycle used to obtain the continuous improvement that is so essential today in our competitive environment.

Chapter 5

Strategic Planning and CSFs

Strategic planning can enable any organization to achieve significant results, or even breakthrough performances in key processes and organizational performance measures. Your strategic planning process will be driven by your customers' voice and by a vision to move the organization forward to higher customer service satisfaction levels. Your vision sets out what you want your organization to be in 10 to 20 years. "We will deliver your packages by 10:30 a.m. tomorrow" sounds normal today, but 20 years ago those few words guided a large corporation (FedEx) in everything that they did. Eventually, that vision became a reality. Later, it became an industry standard.

Your mission describes exactly what your organization does and why it exists. Your vision, mission, and customer voices will drive your strategic planning process. As we've discussed in prior chapters, your key result areas (KRAs)—the areas on which your organization should focus in order to get maximum results—are derived from your vision and mission. Quality, cost, delivery, safety, and productivity are all examples of KRAs. As you'll recall, you can turn your KRAs into both brief and long-range goals simply by adding an action verb, such as *improve, increase, decrease,* etc. Again, your goals have objectives that need to be SMART: specific, measurable, actionable, relevant, and time framed.

But before you formulate your short-term, specific goals, you need to conduct an environmental scan and SWOT analysis (see Chapter 2) and use those results in your planning process.

Your environmental scan will look at what is coming toward your organization from government, the economy, technology, and other external forces. Your SWOT (strengths-weaknesses-opportunities-threats) analysis identifies each and uses them to develop possible objectives. Strengths are used to overcome weaknesses or take advantage of opportunities. Potential threats are dealt with by identifying actions that could reduce the possible risk.

You'll want to ask—and answer—certain key questions during your SWOT analysis, for example: How can we use our strengths to give us an advantage? How can we overcome or minimize the threats? Can our strengths help us to develop new products or services? Can our weaknesses be improved and, if so, how? How are potential governmental regulations going to affect us? Is there anything we are not doing to cope with the changing environment that we should be doing? For example: Should we establish a sales office in a country in which we already have a distribution partner? Can we improve the sales of our products by increasing their quality levels through Six Sigma? How do we reduce our carbon footprint to comply with new environmental regulations? Can we improve our distribution flexibility by increasing our partnerships in this area?

For each goal, you need to develop at least one objective. Again, you need to make it SMART. Don't knock yourself out trying to come up with a first-draft objective that's already SMART. Instead, draft the objective as you normally might and then review the acronym to make it SMART.

For example,

DRAFT   Decrease cycle time at our West Group Plant
SMART   Decrease cycle time by 20% at our Westbrook Plant by December 31, 2008

Notice that the measure and target are included in the objective:

- Measure is cycle time.
- Target is 20% by December 31, 2008.

These measures are the way you'll track how well your strategic plan objectives are achieved. So why isn't "target is 20% by December 31, 2008" a CSF? The answer is that it is your objective: a *target* or *goal* to achieve. CSFs are the *drivers* that will help you achieve it. Your objective is then linked to your vision; in other words, achieving your objective will positively impact your vision. For example, if your vision is to deliver packages by 10:30 a.m. the next day, your objectives will be to increase your airplane flights, increase your distribution facilities, and hire and train good people in order to achieve this vision. Remember that the vision, along with the mission and customer's voice, drives your objective formulation process. Your objectives should support achieving your vision.

When measuring the CSFs and their progress, you need to ensure that your CSFs and objectives are correlated. The assumption is that if CSF progress increases, strategic plan implementation and results, to include attaining your objectives, also increase. Remember that the CSFs are drivers, not an end in and of themselves. You can ensure that your CSFs and objectives are positively correlated by first establishing your objectives and then selecting the CSFs necessary to drive their implementation.

After you develop your performance measures, you next need to identify strategies that will lead to actions. Select the strategy that will be most effective for your particular initiative. If you wanted to improve electric service reliability, for example, you might consider several possible strategies. For example, improving the systems design, enhancing the conductors and poles, reducing response time when electric service is interrupted, and addressing the major causes of an interruption (trees blown into distribution lines, cable failures, lightning, etc.) are all possible strategies. From your list, you need to select the strategy or strategies that most improve customer satisfaction while being cost-effective. If your goal or target is to significantly increase electric service reliability, you'll probably have to pick several strategies to ensure success.

If resources permit, you should appoint a champion for each objective. The champion coordinates with other top managers as necessary, assists in gaining necessary resources, and guides overall objective development and implementation. He or she manages the strategic teams, who in turn develop action plans/implementation plans and execute them upon approval of resources.

Management reviews should be held by top management periodically—every six months or so—and focus on each objective. These reviews should cover progress, barriers, and assistance required, if any, to meet the objective(s). Top management can provide guidance, recommendations, and help eliminate any barriers to progress, if possible.

CSFs to Ensure Strategic Planning Success

Within most organizations, the CSFs best suited for strategic planning are generally the following:

- ■ Top management commitment/support
- ■ Objectives and targets established
- ■ Resources provided
- ■ Measurement
- ■ Champion involvement/leadership
- ■ Communications
- ■ Linkage of objectives to vision
- ■ Executive or management reviews

However, CSFs may vary depending on your organization's size, the complexity of your objectives, the health of your organization, and the maturity of growth.

CSFs are most commonly measured using method 1. As you'll recall from Chapter 4, this method rates each CSF on a scale of 1 to 5, with 1 equaling beginning implementation and 5 equaling completed implementation. Method 1 will be demonstrated in detail in Chapter 7. For the corporate objectives and vision, the corporate metrics will show whether they are being accomplished or improved.

Relationship between KRAs and CSFs in Strategic Planning

Both KRAs and CSFs have an important role in strategic planning. KRAs help develop the long-range goals and ensure that you focus your improvement efforts on the things that are in the organization's best interests. KRAs provide the right linkage and align the corporate arrows in the correct direction, facilitating customer satisfaction.

Key performance indicators (KPIs) are measures that quantify objectives. Key performance indicators, in this case, are simply the performance measures that have been targeted for improvement in the strategic plan.

CSFs identify the areas that *must* be paid attention to ensure the strategic plan is a success. It is possible for a KRA and CSF to be the same; quality improvement and cost are two possible examples (see Figure 5.1). As I emphasized in Chapter 3, it is important to note that their *purpose* differs, depending upon whether they are a KRA or a CSF.

CSFs are an integral part of the strategic planning process. They must be achieved if your organization is to show either incremental or breakthrough improvement (Figure 5.2).

Figure 5.1 Aligning the vectors.

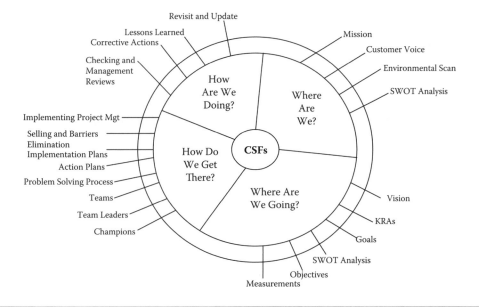

Figure 5.2 Progress is not made unless the CSFs are being achieved.

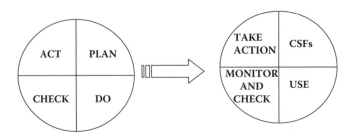

Figure 5.3 PDCA.

Remember our PDCA cycle? Identify the CSFs early, measure them, monitor progress, and take action when needed. In the plan phase, identify the CSFs and their measures. In the do phase, implement the CSFs. In the check phase, monitor and check their implementation progress. In the act phase, take corrective actions to get them back on track (Figure 5.3).

Let's take a look at this in practice.

Example: A Barbershop

A small business, a barbershop, opens in a well-visited mall. Its mission and vision has been consolidated into: "To become the best barbershop in this neighborhood by providing the best haircut and shaves to our customers, with 97% customer satisfaction and 99% return rates."

Its strategic goals are:

■ Achieve high customer satisfaction
■ Retain existing customers and attract new ones
■ Provide timely and quality barber services
■ Be the first choice for barber services and products in the neighborhood
■ Make a profit

These goals are broad and long range. They set the stage for developing more specific objectives, while linking directly to the shop's vision/mission.

The strategic SMART objectives established by the stakeholders, owners, and hired barbers are:

1. No one has to wait longer than fifteen minutes prior to being served.
2. There is adequate sitting room available for at least fifteen people to wait.

3. Gain local market share of 51% by the end of 2008.
4. Obtain and sustain a customer satisfaction rate of 97% or higher during the first year.

The vision/mission, goals, and objectives provide the foundation that enables them to identify what is critical in order that they may be achieved. To achieve their objectives, our barbershop's management team needs to follow the process we've already outlined in Chapter 4. To recap:

Step 1: Define goals, objectives, policy, systems, vision/mission, etc., you want to accomplish or implement.

Step 2: Identify potential CSFs. Brainstorming or green lighting are popular choices to identify potential CSFs. Sometimes listing the objectives in the left-hand column of a chart and then identifying what is critical to achieve them in the right-hand column can be a useful technique. Once all objectives have been scrutinized, look at the goals and vision/mission statement to make sure nothing important was overlooked.

In our example, the stakeholders (including owners and barbers) identified the following objectives and possible CSFs:

Objectives	Potential CSFs
1. No one has to wait longer than 15 minutes.	• Accurate customer service staffing model (right number of barbers to match customer demand)
	• Right number of barber's chairs
2. There is adequate sitting room available for at least 15 people waiting.	• Sufficient chairs, benches, etc., to sit 15 people comfortably
3. Gain local market share of 51% by end of 2008.	• Attract new clients/customers by increasing competitiveness vs. other local barbershops
	• Be able to expand if needed (finances, space, etc.)
4. Obtain and sustain a customer satisfaction rate of 97% or higher.	• Excellent customer service; good-natured, competent barbers

Step 3: Evaluate and select the critical factors. Now that we have identified several potential CSFs, our next step is to identify only those that are critical to achieving the vision/mission (see Figure 5.4, where we'll turn vision into action.)

Step 4: List the key elements/subfactors for each factor.

CSFs	Subfactors of the CSFs
Correct staffing	• Barber/customer ratio
	• Competent in latest haircuts
	• Customer focused
	• Patient
	• Good work habits
Attract new customers	• Quality of haircuts and shaves
	• Advertisement: Paid, word of mouth
	• Waiting time and comfort of waiting
	• Perceived value: What customers received vs. what they expected to receive
Provide excellent customer service	• Friendly
	• Courteous
	• Quick service
	• Empathy
	• Remembers how customers want their hair cut

Step 5: Determine the performance measures for each CSF selected. For correct staffing, a critical staffing indicator could be developed or an alternate, less costly measure could be used. "Correct staffing" is to have a barber ready to serve a customer without the customer waiting more than fifteen minutes. Average or maximum wait times could both be used as indicators for this CSF.

A login by customers on a form, to subsequently be filled out by the barber when the customer is served, could provide the data for this indicator.

Attracting new customers can be simply measured by tracking the total number of customers served daily (accumulate for a month, and graph). The trend upward (good) or downward (bad) will show how you are doing.

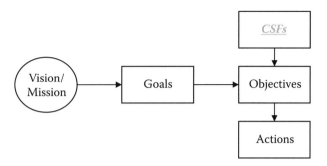

Potential CSFs	Critical?	Remarks
1. Accurate Customer Service Model	Necessary but not critical	Can be calculated manually as needed.
2. Right Number of Competent Barbers and Barber Chairs (Correct Staffing)	Critical	Essential for attracting new customers and minimizing wait time.
3. Sufficient Chairs, Benches, etc., to Sit Comfortably 15 People	Necessary, but one time occurrence	Once done, it does not have to be counted for performance or implementation progress.
4. Attract New Clients/ Customer	Yes, critical	Attract by increasing competitiveness is an action or strategy, not a CSF.
5. Be Able to Expand if Needed	Not critical now, but could become critical in the future	Adequate size now but as market share gains, could become critical.
6. Provide Excellent Customer Service	Critical	A must to achieve customer satisfaction, retain customers, and attract new ones (See #2).
7. Retain Staff and Maintain Their Customer Focus	Necessary but not critical at this time	Could become a problem. Competent staff available now.

Figure 5.4   Vision to actions.

The "provide excellent customer service," CSF can be measured by a customer service index. A customer satisfaction survey (administered on-site) could be used. If the customers put their telephone numbers on the sign-in log, the barbershop can send a survey by mail. Both of these methods are good measures, but are costly for a barbershop. Our barbershop could use a simple, creative method for measuring customer satisfaction, such as keeping white and red poker chips by the door and a box to put them in. A sign above the box might read: "Please put in a white chip in the box if you are pleased with the service you received,

Figure 5.5   Customer satisfaction graph for the barbershop.

or a red one if you are dissatisfied with any dimension of the service."
The barbershop's management can accumulate the chips daily, add
them together, and graph the total each month (see Figure 5.5).

Step 6: Monitor and take action. Track your CSFs *at least* monthly. You
could also track them weekly or biweekly, and when the trend is going
the wrong way on any of the three measures, identify the root causes
and then take corrective measures to eliminate or at least minimize
them. The frequency of monitoring is dictated by how quickly you'll
need to take corrective action to ensure that your objective implementation is on track.

Communicate the CSFs to all stakeholders and how you are measuring
them. It will foster focus on what is really important. That's what CSFs
are all about—achieving what is critical to be successful.

This six-step process can be applied to almost any initiative that your
organization undertakes. Whatever your objective, CSFs can help you successfully implement it.

In Chapter 6, we'll go into more detail on measuring and monitoring CSFs
and taking corrective action as needed.

A Systems Example Using CSFs: ISO 14001

Systems implementation is a normal happening at midsize and large organizations, and can even be common in some small businesses. Implementing a system is a business improvement, and CSFs can play a major role in ensuring that systems are implemented correctly and on time. By now, you know what a CSF is, how to identify possible CSFs, and how to select CSFs for an improvement project. Now it's time to enhance your ability to measure CSF implementation progress and address any barriers that you encounter. Later the CSFs will be identified for this system implementation, measured, and used to improve progress and results.

Let's say that you've selected ISO 14001, which outlines environmental management system (EMS) development and implementation, to be implemented at your plant or facility. ISO 14001 consists of five phases: an environmental policy, planning, implementation and operation, checking and corrective action, and management reviews. Each phase, other than the policy and management review, has several elements that must be accomplished effectively:

1. Policy, which counts as both a phase and an element
2. Planning
   Elements:
   - Aspects and impacts
   - Legal and other requirements
   - Objectives and targets
   - Environmental management programs

3. Implementation and operation
    Elements:
    - Structure and responsibility
    - Training, awareness, and competence
    - Communication
    - EMS documentation
    - Document control
    - Operations control
    - Emergency preparedness and response
4. Checking and corrective action
    Elements:
    - Monitoring and measurement
    - Nonconformance and corrective and preventative action
    - Records
    - EMS audit
5. Management review, which counts as both a phase and an element

Before we go any further, let's define EMS. An EMS is a set of processes designed to improve the environmental performance of any organization. It starts with identifying all of the environmental aspects of a process, and then identifying *how* they impact the environment, for example, by polluting the air, polluting the water, going to a landfill, or contaminating the soil.

Next, we want to rank how much each of these aspects impacts the environment. We can assign criteria to each aspect, such as scale of impact and probability of occurrence, and weight the aspects accordingly. Each aspect will be scored against the criteria using a 1 to 5 scale; 1 constitutes a low impact, and 5 is a high impact. The aspects with the highest scores are significant. Once we've identified these high-impact aspects, we can create objectives and targets to lessen their impact.

The above list illustrates the five phases, with seventeen elements comprising the EMS. "Objectives and targets" is a good example. These are the things that you have targeted for improvement, which will (or should) drive implementation and lead to improved environmental performance. Some of the elements may also be drivers to the development and implementation of an EMS, such as communications and training. All will have to be accomplished to achieve full implementation of an EMS and continual improvement of environmental performance.

Other elements that are *not* critical success factors, such as documentation, will get done if the CSFs are implemented and achieved. Some of the CSFs that make this happen are top management commitment, employee involvement, and resources provided. They are not EMS elements, but are critical to EMS's success.

The Selected CSFs

Not long ago, I was assigned as a facilitator to several organizations wishing to develop and implement EMS. First, we identified our CSFs. Several cross-functional EMS teams used multivoting to select, from a list of fifty possible CSFs that I had identified, the CSFs critical to the development and implementation of an EMS at their organization. They selected top management commitment, employee involvement, communications, objectives and targets, integrated into daily work, and management reviews/continual improvement (teamwork was also added at a couple of locations). The CSFs selected include three of the seventeen elements. Note that all three are drivers of *actions*: objectives and targets, communication, and management reviews. The successful achievement of the seven selected CSFs is critical in ensuring that all seventeen elements are accomplished and the desired results achieved. Different EMS teams may select slightly different CSFs, but most will be similar. Organizational difference, the scope of implementation, previous members' experiences, the organization leadership, whether ISO 9000 has been implemented previously, and other key characteristics (such as the degree of compliance) can lead to some different selections. Projects, discipline and consequences, proven methods, teamwork, procedures, and effective change management are examples that could easily be selected for EMS development and implementation.

Top management commitment and communications will always be selected as CSFs for systems implementation. Again, regardless of what CSFs are selected, they must be measurable and periodically evaluated, and actions must be taken if they are not on course to achieve the desired results. CSF improvement plans can be developed simply by observing where you are and considering the next level's activities. If the CSFs are implemented and managed, then both the CSFs and ISO 14001 EMS will improve (Figure 6.1). Remember that these seven CSFs are vital to the successful implementation of the five phases and seventeen elements of ISO 14001 EMS.

Measuring the CSFs

Our CSF implementation team selected measurement method 1, stages to implementation (as discussed in Chapter 4), to use for measuring their CSFs.

CSF	Action
Employee involvement	• Start recycling
	• Train employees on their needed contributions
Top management commitment	• Conduct system orientation training
	• Solicit their ideas

Figure 6.1 Example of a CSF improvement plan.

As you'll recall, this method shows progress along the way. When one of the CSFs is not keeping up (staying at a low level, from 1 to 3, while others are increasing), the team develops actions to improve it. Improving CSF implementation is generally a simple procedure. The team looks at the description for the next level and then determines what has to happen to get there. These actions or events become their plan. To start this method, determine what the CSF looks like prior to improvement—this gets a score of 1. Next, what does the CSF look like when it is fully achieved? That gets the maximum score of 5. Then fill in three other areas, determining step-wise progress from 2 to 4, since 1 and 5 have already been defined. Starting with 2, it shows progress from 1; 2 shows progress to 3; etc. At the end of the month, each team member scores each CSF. The scores for each CSF are calculated, and the total actual score is determined by adding up all the CSF scores and dividing by the number of people scoring the CSFs' progress. The total possible score is the number of CSFs times 5. In the above case, 7 CSFs × 5 = 35. For example:

Total Score Determination					
CSF	*January*	*February*	*March*	*April*	*May*
Top management commitment	1 (the average of five people scoring it)	1.5	2	2	3
Employee involvement	1	1	1.5	1.5	1.5
Communications	1	1	1	2	2
Resources Provided	1	1	1	1.5	1.5
Objectives and targets	1	1.5	2	2	3
Integrate into daily work	1	1	1	1	2

continued

CSF	January	February	March	April	May
Teamwork	2	2	2.5	3	3
Total score	8 of 35	9 of 35	11 of 35	13 of 35	16 of 35
Team members participating	5	5	5	6	6
Plot for graph	1.6	1.8	2.2	2.16	2.67

A graph (preferably a line graph, since it best illustrates trends in data) should be plotted monthly. The trend will show improvement or not. Either the score or a percentage can be measured (y axis). The x axis should be time in months. See Figure 6.2.

Each individual CSF can also be plotted monthly (see Figure 6.3). Together, all the individual graphs show how the total CSFs' monthly score (Figure 6.2) evolved. The scores or ratings come from the rating sheet, developed by the author, administered monthly to the facility environmental management system team.

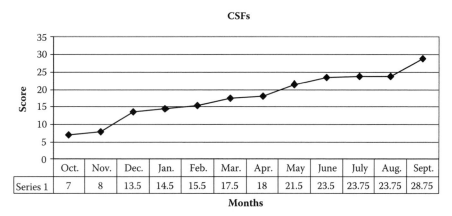

	Oct.	Nov.	Dec.	Jan.	Feb.	Mar.	Apr.	May	June	July	Aug.	Sept.
Series 1	7	8	13.5	14.5	15.5	17.5	18	21.5	23.5	23.75	23.75	28.75

Figure 6.2   CSFs graph.

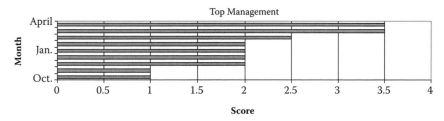

Figure 6.3   Top management commitment.

I. Top management commitment (1–5) _____
   1 Not involved or at least not visible to employees of involvement
   2 Approved the program, does talk the talk sometimes
   3 Chairs or participates in some meetings, gives verbal support
   4 Involved, shows commitment, provides support and resources
   5 Very committed; walks the talk, asks for updates, chairs management reviews, provides budget and resources

II. Employee involvement (1–5) _____
   1 Most not aware of EMS and environmental performance
   2 Only those who work with significant aspects are involved
   3 A large number of volunteers to help in programs such as recycling is occurring
   4 Recycling is a success; seems most are involved
   5 Almost everyone is involved in some environmental efforts; results and continual environmental improvement have been achieved; everyone follows guidelines and processes are being performed safely and with excellent results; environment is everyone's business; world-class performance

III. Communications (1–5) _____
   1 Little, if any, communications on EMS
   2 Less than 10% know what the environmental policy is
   3. At least one communication media used and 50% or more know what the environmental policy and EMS is
   4 More than 80% know what the environmental policy includes and what EMS is trying to accomplish; more than one communication media is used
   5 Everyone is aware of the environmental policy, EMS, organization's objectives and target, and how we are doing; examples of communication media: telephone, email with attachments, newsletter, letters, staff meetings, town hall meetings, procedures, pamphlets, handouts, bulletin boards, etc.

IV. Objectives and targets (1–5) _____
   1 None developed
   2 Doing aspects and impacts
   3 Preliminary objectives developed
   4 Management environmental programs developed
   5 MEPs have been developed, resources approved, and implementation has begun

V. Resources/budget (1–5) _____
   1 No resources provided
   2 Resources have been requested
   3 Some funds/resources have been provided
   4 Sufficient resources are available for all EMPs
   5 Separate budget with more than adequate funds
VI. Integrated into daily work (1–5) _____
   1 People unaware of what is needed to be done
   2 A lot of people aware of EMS; have begun to get involved
   3 Eighty percent or more are cognizant and trying to do what is needed
   4 Processes performed very well and most waste is recycled
   5 Everyone understands the environment is all of our concern and
      their involvement and support reflects this every day; EMS is totally
      integrated; environmental performance has significantly improved
      and continual improvement is occurring
VII. Management reviews/continual improvement (1–5) _____
   1 Management review team not in place; no improvement
   2 Team formed, duties outlined, no meetings yet
   3 Management review team meeting—at least once; CARs (Corrective
      Action Reports) written
   4 Some improvement documented
   5 Management review team meeting at least twice a year; major
      improvements have been achieved; continual improvement is an
      organization vision and the overall environmental performance
      continues to get better

   See Figure 6.4 for a graph of the CSF performance.
   The actual data (monthly CSF composite score) is plotted monthly
using a solid line. If the EMS is being implemented successfully, this
line will increase monthly and eventually, after about one year, become
stable, after the system has completed one plan-do-check-act cycle. This
means that the execution has gone from the planning and development
cycle into one of *maintaining* the EMS. The CSFs for maintaining the
EMS could vary slightly from those selected for planning and implementation. Therefore, when entering the maintain phase, you should
do another assessment to ascertain what is critical to ensuring success
in maintaining your EMS. The answers will probably be the same or
similar. The structure of the EMS is in place, but environmental aspects
will still be reviewed, and new objectives and targets will be developed
for continual improvement.

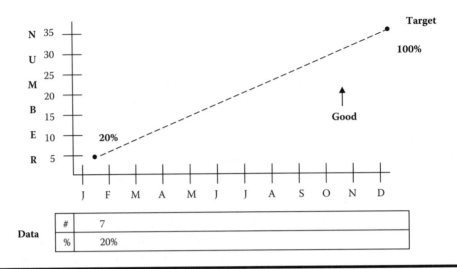

Figure 6.4 CSF progress: EMS implementation.

Management must be sure that there are some sustaining factors in place to ensure continuation. A policy, requirement, reviews, and audits are excellent examples of why an organization needs to continue holding meetings, developing and completing objectives and targets, and improving their EMS and the organization's environmental performance.

Continuous improvement is essential to EMS. An excellent technique to assist in this pursuit is benchmarking with a progressive organization that has been very successful in its own EMS efforts. In Chapter 7, we'll explore this technique.

Chapter 7

Benchmarking and CSFs

Benchmarking Overview

So far, we've discussed how you can use the CSF method to identify and monitor the factors critical to your organization's success. We've talked about using CSFs to advance your strategic plan, and in the last chapter, you saw how that can look in real terms. In this chapter, I'll provide you with another tool for your toolkit: benchmarking.

If you're not too familiar with benchmarking, it might initially seem like nothing more than copying what other organizations do. On the contrary, benchmarking can be an excellent tool for significantly improving the performance of your organization's key processes. Benchmarking is an established process with several steps that, if followed, should enable your organization to increase its performance to best-in-class or world-class performance levels.

Benchmarking starts with the objective of improving a process. To improve your process, you want to find someone who really does it well and learn from him or her. Prior to reviewing the other organization's process, your organization needs to develop a plan. Too often, companies or organizations rush to the other organization's site to observe, but without a plan, you won't come back with the fix needed to improve your process. All that happened was that your organization's group took a field trip. Here's how to benchmark: you need to decide *what* to benchmark and *who* to benchmark; then you need to benchmark, capture the changes needed, and adapt the process to your organization.

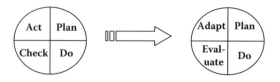

Figure 7.1 Benchmarking model.

The benchmarking process, depending on which author you read, can range from just a few steps to a fourteen-step process.[11] It is helpful to think of it as another tool based on the Deming wheel, PDCA (plan-do-check-act) (Figure 7.1).

The steps can be described by the four phases plan, do, evaluate, and adapt. The steps are outlined below:

Plan
1. Decide to benchmark: Establish a benchmarking team; train and support the team. The benchmarking team should be familiar with what needs improvement. They should also receive some benchmarking training. Top management should write and publish a charter that spells out the objective, their expectations, rules if needed, team composition, champion of the area, and any other information deemed pertinent.
2. Determine process for improvement: The team needs to identify, through metrics research, problem analysis, or guidance from management, the process or activity in the process to be improved.
3. Understand the process—activities, measures, outputs, inputs, outcome, and characteristics: Using the SIPOOC process, the team should identify the suppliers' inputs, activities, and measures; the activities and measures of the process (where the work or value is added or done); the outputs (information, a product, or service); the outcome (efficiency, productivity, dollars in profit); and customers (external customers who receive the outputs). Once the team has compiled this information, they can create a process flowchart to identify specifics that need to be improved.
4. Select the measure(s) to improve. From the above flowchart, identify the progress or outcome metrics (or both) that measure the activities targeted for improvement.
5. Study and select organization to benchmark. From conducting a literature review, using a benchmarking warehouse, or doing an industry search, identify companies that perform your targeted areas very well.

6. Arrange for a site visit and reach a benchmarking agreement between the selected company and your organization. Benchmarking is especially effective if you can manage to complete this. It is not easy, but well worth the effort. Normally, the company or organization you benchmark with wants something in turn for helping you. You will need to negotiate and be sure you can deliver what they desire.

Do

7. Go to site, observe process, interview key people, and take notes about similarities and differences. Yogi Berra said, "You can see a lot just by observing." Your team members are observers. Be sure they have specific areas they are looking for so that no time is wasted and all essential information and data are gathered.

8. Flowchart the high performing process, using the simple symbols in Visio or a simpler flowcharting template.

Evaluate

9. Study the benchmarked process against the process that the team wishes to improve. Highlight what is different and the best practices. Formulate a new process and test it by checking all activities and their flow. Be sure needed activities are included and the activity sequence is logical.

Adapt

10. Put together an implementation plan to include coordination, communication, changeover plan, etc. Pinpoint who is going to do what, when, and where.

11. Brief all involved change work assignments, schedule, job classifications and descriptions. Be sure human resources, the champion of the benchmarking effort, the process owner, and all process members are involved. All parties need to fully understand all aspects of what is going to happen, why, and the benefits sought.

12. Pilot if large, install if medium or small. If you plan to replicate the change in several locations, try it in one location first and work out the bugs. Remember Murphy's Law: "If something can go wrong, it will." Once all the problems are worked out, work instructions developed, and personnel knowledgeable of their new duties, it is time to replicate, and reap the benefits at all locations where these activities are done within the organization. Provide oversight: In other words, handle any problems that occur, measure performance, keep everyone involved, etc.

The steps above provide a simple overview of benchmarking. (See Camp[11] for more comprehensive coverage.) Benchmarking is a process. When the team picks a process to improve, this endeavor then becomes a project. As such, a project plan with milestones should be developed and used in executing the project.

There are two possibilities for using CSFs during the benchmarking process. The first CSF application is conducting the benchmarking itself. The second possibility is using CSFs for the pilot and replication of the new process.

CSFs for Benchmarking

CSFs can be very helpful when used in benchmarking. Some are obvious, such as:

- Top management commitment/support
- Teaming
- Communications
- Resources
- Training

But others could also come into play, such as best practices, employee involvement, information, innovation, integrated into daily work, management involvement, productivity, objectives and targets, roles and responsibility, safety, and technology.

Under most circumstances, you'd use the bulleted list as your CSFs for benchmarking, and select one or two others, depending on the purpose and complexity of the benchmark sought.

Benchmarking itself may be identified as a CSF critical to the effort being undertaken. For example, IBM uses IPD (Integrated Product Development) to get to the market faster, more efficiently, and most of all, with products that meet or exceed customers' requirements. Key components of their process are market and competitor knowledge, teams working together cross-functionally, and using the customer voice in the design and production of their products. Five CSFs drive this process:[12]

- Executive support—Leadership, resources support, providing focus.
- Communications—Communicate purpose to all and provide training of why, what, when, where, and how to accomplish.

- Customer focus—Market driven.
- Building one team—Teamwork, cross-functional but with same goals.
- Benchmarking—Adopting best practices and improving performance.

Why is benchmarking one of IBM's CSFs? The purpose of benchmarking is to improve a process. In this instance, IBM's initiative is to improve product development. Benchmarking can help to do that.

Measuring the CSFs

The benchmarking team should settle on about five to eight CSFs. Next, they'll need to select the measure from the table below.

Seven Possible Methods to Measure CSF Implementation		
Method	*Title*	*When to Use*
Method 1	Start to finish implementation	Project goes through stages; method measures progress from start to finish
Method 2	Critical success level	When a critical success level such as a sales goal is important to the initiative's success
Method 3	SMART objectives	Making an objective measurable by putting a measure as part of the objective statement
Method 4	Traditional industry measures	Most industries have some common measures, such as 90% of customers' calls answered in three rings or less
Method 5	Traffic light	When data are not available, but performance can be described by words such as *red* (poor performance), *yellow* (needs improvement), and *green* (good performance)
Method 6	Surveys	Surveys are good to collect information at a point in time, such as starting an initiative and then at the end; the difference would show amount of improvement
Method 7	Scatter approach	When several related measures are available and all can be used to measure progress or change; normally, just one available measure does not provide full coverage; by using more than one measure, additional coverage is obtained

Objective CSFs—Measure—Monitor—Take action

Figure 7.2 CSFs simplified model.

Measurement methods 1 to 3 may all be relevant to this particular initiative. The important thing is to measure the CSF implementation progress and results achieved.

Using the model shown in Figure 7.2, the final measure of success is, "Did the process performance indicator selected actually improve, and did it achieve the target?"

Benchmarking is an excellent technique to improve your processes and organizational performance. If you decide to benchmark, identifying the CSFs for accomplishing the benchmark and implementing them can help you achieve success.

Chapter 8

Critical Success Measures for Process Success

Everyone reading this book is familiar with the concept of work, but have you ever thought about what you do to complete work? Simply put, work is accomplished by performing activities in a process. A process is a sequence of activities that produce a product, service, or information through inputs, outputs, and outcomes (Figure 8.1). The point of process improvement is to improve the output or outcome of the process. Often, especially for small businesses, we have to *develop* a process in order to undertake an initiative, rather than simply improve an existing one. In both cases, the use of CSFs will help. In this chapter, we'll talk about using CSFs in process improvement.

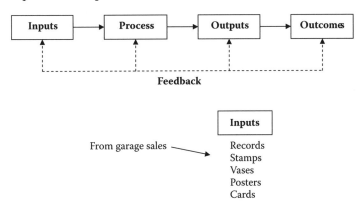

Figure 8.1   A process diagram.

Inputs are utilized in the process to produce the product, service, or information. Inputs can include labor, machinery, electricity, sensors, money, equipment, raw materials, and so on.

Examples of product outputs include cars, computers, furniture, TVs, stereos, dishes, plates, and batteries. Service outputs can include waiting on a customer, answering a telephone, serving coffee, driving a taxi, or delivering a package. Information outputs can include reports, magazines, and presentations.

Outcomes result when a customer receives the product(s), service, or information. Favorable outcomes might be a satisfied or excited customer, reliable or quick service, timely delivery, accurate or useful information, and coming in on or under budget. Unfavorable outcomes could include rework, unhappy customers, errors, rejects, bad information, and coming in over budget.

The process takes the inputs and transforms them into a product, service, or information that causes an outcome (some favorable and some not). Of course, all organizations want their processes to produce quality products, services, or information that results in favorable outcomes.

Process Example

To see how processes should work, let's take a look at Jim, who's just lost his job as a computer salesman. Jim knows sales and computers. After several interviews, Jim became worried about finding a new job in computers. During his interviews, he invariably discovered that he was either too experienced or did not meet the organization's job requirements, would've had to travel too much, or the pay was inadequate, all of which led him to worry about his future. He decided to start his own business, and given his skills set, selling on eBay seemed to be an excellent option.

For his process to be successful, Jim knew that he would first need inputs for selling on eBay. He brainstormed possibilities and determined that he would need to use his car, with a tank full of gas, and some cash in small bills, to go to garage sales (Figure 8.2).

Next, he had to know how to sell his merchandise (inputs) on eBay. He needed a digital camera (another input) to take pictures of his product. Jim knew how to use the computer and the Internet and how to type. Therefore, no training (input) was needed for him to start the process. After

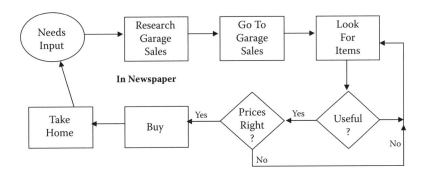

Figure 8.2   The process for gathering items.

Jim acquired some items he thought he could sell, he was ready. Jim felt that his CSFs were:

- Sufficient inventory of saleable products
- Good presentation of his products on eBay
- Timely packaging and shipping of his sales
- Excellent customer service (honesty regarding the condition of his products, timely answers to emails requesting more information, etc.)

See Figure 8.3 for a map of the selling process and customers' satisfaction.

Critical-to-Success Measures

Jim has defined his process. He knows that to make a living off of eBay, he will need to sell enough items to bring in at least $800 a week in profit. His average income (sales – cost) per item is $20, so Jim will need to sell at least forty items a week, with the buyer paying for the mailing. So Jim has identified an important outcome measure, or critical success level (since Jim has to make that much money to meet his expenses). Also, he wants positive feedback from his customers so he can stay in business. Figure 8.4 summarizes the measures.

Jim knows he has to sell, mail, and receive payment for at least forty items per week, and must gather at least that amount or more in his supply inventory to be ready for the next week. To track the elements that are critical to his success measure—making enough money to pay the bills—Jim has set up a simple measurement system. These are Jim's success measures.

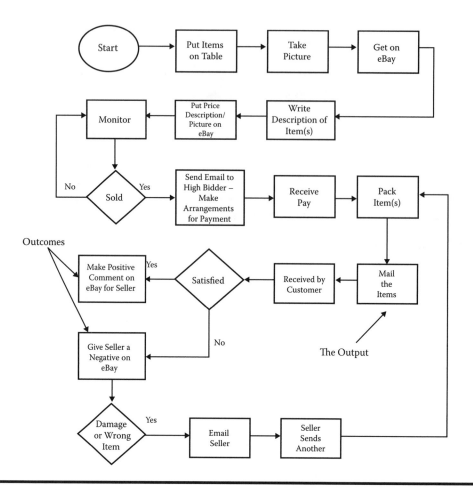

Figure 8.3   The selling process and customers' satisfaction.

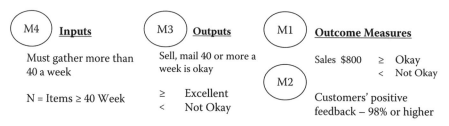

Figure 8.4   Important measures critical to Jim's success.

Remember our measurement models from Chapter 4? Sales per week are a measure of type 3, SMART objectives, discussed previously in Chapter 4. Customer satisfaction is an industry measure (method 4). Measures 3 (outputs) and 4 (outcomes) are critical levels. (See method 2, critical levels, in Chapter 4.)

It is often possible to use more than one measurement technique per application. Measurement methods 1, implementation, and 3, making

Figure 8.5 CSFs and measures.

	Items Bought	Items On eBay	Items Sold	Items Mailed	$ Sales – Cost
Week 1	75	45	40	40	$820
Week 2	40	48	42	40	$795
Week 3	92	70	60	55	$910
Week 4	33	42	36	35	$690
Week 5	35	44	40	40	$755
Week 6	60	51	48	48	$890
Total	335	300	266	258	$4,860

Figure 8.6 Six weeks of business data.

objectives SMART, are often used together. As shown in Figure 8.5, Jim has combined measurement methods 2, critical success levels, 3, making objectives SMART, and 4, traditional industry measures, to illustrate the measures critical to Jim's success (often called measures of success).

Jim's business data after six weeks are shown in Figure 8.6.

Figure 8.7 shows that, for the six weeks Jim has been in business, three weeks have been above the target and three have been below. So how did Jim do? When we divide his total sales ($4,860) by six weeks, he's averaging $810. Overall, not bad. Is our indicator the best measure? No, the cumulative average tells us more. See Figure 8.8.

The sales average indicator shows that every week but one, the average was above $800, and was below $800 for the other week. The averages were almost all on target, since only 16 are below the $810 average. How is Jim doing? Okay, as far as sales go.

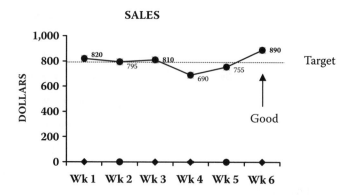

Figure 8.7   Sales per week.

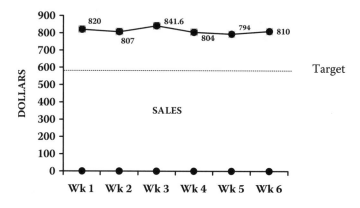

Figure 8.8   Sales average.

But Jim is not doing as well in meeting the customers' needs. His eBay rating is only 92.5, rather than his targeted 98. What can Jim do? What does Figure 8.9 show?

Jim needs to increase his customers' satisfaction. Customers are why he is in business, and retaining them will keep him in business. A high rating will also encourage new customers to buy his products. First, Jim will need to focus on improving shipping. This corrective action alone, if successful, will enable him to achieve his 98% customer satisfaction goal. Jim needs to improve the late shipments, then address the items not as advertised, then those broken/damaged.

Figure 8.10 shows the number of items sold and mailed. Jim sold and mailed more than forty each week, except for week 4. His average is forty-three sold and mailed each week.

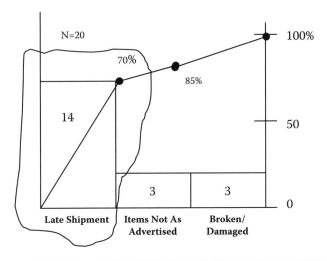

Figure 8.9   Pareto chart of Jim's customer complaints.

Jim's goal is to gather forty items or more a week. He may need to set an inventory ceiling and manage to keep below it while having sufficient inventory to maintain his business. Otherwise, he may have to rent space and incur additional overhead costs that would necessitate selling more items to reach his income target.

Recap of the Type of Measures Used

Four performance measures were identified and demonstrated in the six-week example. These measures are shown in Figure 8.10.

Measures originate from processes, or their inputs, outputs, or outcomes, or from objectives[11] (see Figure 8.11).

The measure's location is shown in the macro process diagram. Let's look at the job process diagram, which I've expanded to show the major activities and the flow between the activities (Figure 8.12). The measures are shown where they occur.

Measurement is essential to process performance, whether your goal is to maintain or improve that performance. The same holds for a system, since it incorporates several processes that together produce a desired product or service. Going from one process to several will not change the way you determine and use measures. For a system, you'll simply look at the outputs and outcomes from all of the processes instead of just one (see Figure 8.13).

	Week 1	Week 2	Week 3	Week 4	Week 5	Week 6	Total
Items Sold	40	42	60	36	40	48	266
Items Mailed	40	40	55	35	40	48	258
Items Sold and Not Mailed	0	2	5	1	0	0	8

How is Jim doing in obtaining sufficient items to sell? Here are the numbers:

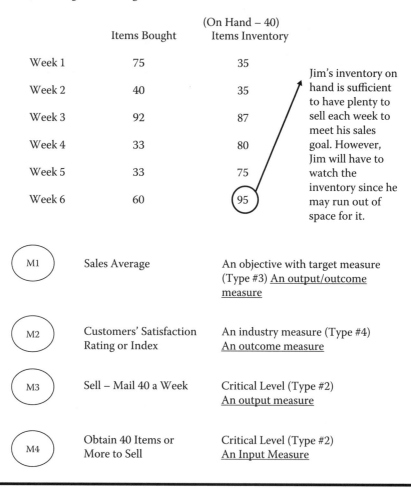

	Items Bought	(On Hand – 40) Items Inventory
Week 1	75	35
Week 2	40	35
Week 3	92	87
Week 4	33	80
Week 5	33	75
Week 6	60	95

Jim's inventory on hand is sufficient to have plenty to sell each week to meet his sales goal. However, Jim will have to watch the inventory since he may run out of space for it.

M1	Sales Average	An objective with target measure (Type #3) <u>An output/outcome measure</u>
M2	Customers' Satisfaction Rating or Index	An industry measure (Type #4) <u>An outcome measure</u>
M3	Sell – Mail 40 a Week	Critical Level (Type #2) <u>An output measure</u>
M4	Obtain 40 Items or More to Sell	Critical Level (Type #2) <u>An Input Measure</u>

Figure 8.10   Items sold and mailed.

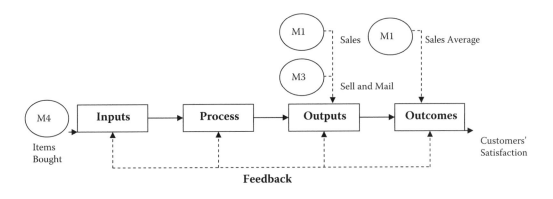

Figure 8.11 A process diagram: Where in the process are the four measures?

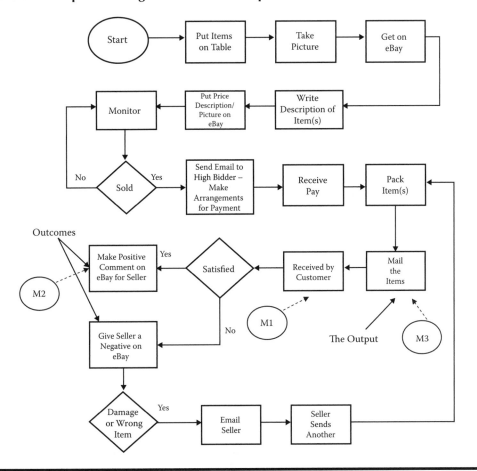

Figure 8.12 The selling process and customers' satisfaction included measures M1, M2, and M3.

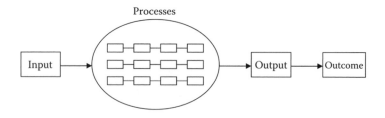

Figure 8.13   A system diagram.

Again, identifying the CSFs, measuring their progress, checking their status, and taking corrective actions will help Jim succeed in his new business endeavor. Here, again, are Jim's CSFs:

- CSF 1: sufficient inventory of saleable products
- CSF 2: Good presentation of his products on eBay
- CSF 3: Timely packaging and shipping of his sales
- CSF 4: Excellent customer service (honesty regarding the condition of his products, timely answers to emails requesting more information, etc.)

Did Jim achieve these CSFs? Jim felt that his second CSF, good presentation of his products on eBay, would not need a specific measure, since if the products sold, that in itself would be an excellent indicator that this CSF was achieved. Measure M 1 does measure CSF 2 to some extent. Measure M 4 tracks how well CSF 1 is being achieved. Measure M 3 shows how well CSF 3 is being achieved. Measure M 2 very effectively measures CSF 4's progress and results. These measures and their corresponding CSFs are summarized as follows:

CSFs	Measures
CSF 1: Sufficient inventory of saleable products	M4
CSF 2: Good presentation of his products on eBay	M1
CSF 3: Pack and ship his sales in a timely manner	M3
CSF 4: Provide excellent customer service (Honesty regarding condition of his products, timely answers to emails asking for more information, etc.)	M4

In summary, the CSF attainment model works well for Jim. It will also work for you to improve your processes' performance or to ensure they are meeting output goals and quality standards.

Your data and goals will be different, but this method provides you with a measurable path to success in improving your processes. By using CSFs, you can improve your processes, and ultimately, your bottom line. Define your improvement purpose first and identify and select your CSFs. Measure them periodically and use the results to take corrective action, if needed.

The same principles and method used for processes can be used to improve job performance and individual improvement pursuits. We'll talk about that in the next two chapters.

Chapter 9

Improving Job Performance through CSFs

So far, we've discussed how to use CSFs to improve processes within your organization and to augment your strategic plan. But an organization is only as good as the people who work in it, and CSFs can be an excellent method for communicating responsibilities and improving and tracking job performance. In identifying CSFs for a job, you first need to determine if there is a need to increase the performance levels of the job. In other words, what is our objective? Depending on your objective(s), different factors may emerge. You need both specific information about the job and a clear objective before you can establish CSFs for improving job performance.

Gathering the Information

Let's start with the job description: What functions, activities, or tasks are performed? What equipment or machinery is needed to perform the tasks, activities, or functions? Is the job a one-person job or a multiperson job? What are the standards for acceptable (or good or great) job performance (if any)? What has the past performance been like? What seems to be the problem, if performance is poor? What education or training is needed? How would you define competence?

If a problem exists, you'll need to create a cause-and-effect diagram (see Figure 9.1).

As Figure 9.2 shows, any given job can be impacted by multiple elements.

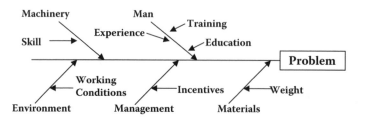

Figure 9.1   Cause-and-effect diagram.

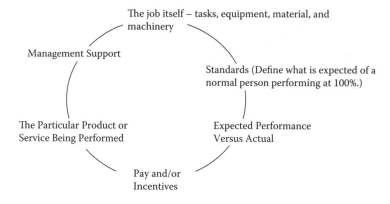

Figure 9.2   Factors affecting job.

Determining the CSFs

The critical success factors will depend on the objective or the job role key result areas (KRAs). Remember, key result areas are thrusts or major focuses in this case for improving the job. To improve performance, the best method to determine the CSFs is:

1. Understand the job
2. Define the objective or roles
3. Brainstorm and prioritize what it will take to achieve the objective or role
4. Assess what may be needed for improvement, for example, additional training or clearer expectations
5. Identify the CSFs needed to make these improvements happen and increase employee performance

Once you have identified items to improve, ask the involved employees for their opinion. Verify that the actions planned for improvement will actually do that and whether or not the CSFs selected seem appropriate.

Example: A Blackjack Dealer

Let's look at a blackjack dealer as an example. A blackjack dealer's day-to-day job is to deal blackjack, handle bets (poker chips), observe the players and ensure honesty, play his or her hand, know when to draw cards and when to fold, pay off winners, gather chips from the losers, and maintain harmony at the table. For each activity, let's take a look at the reason the blackjack dealer does it.

Step 1: Understand the job.

 Playing poker: Why? Customers want to, and casinos make money.

 Customer relations: Why? Treat the customer as king, and keep them coming back.

 Maintaining harmony/managing conflict: Why? Play is smooth and uninterrupted.

 Dealing cards, fast and accurate: Why? More deals equals more money.

 Keeping up with multiple players: Why? More players equals more money.

All the skills could be improved by training. Some training is essential to perform the job, and dealers will need a high school diploma or higher.

Step 2: Define the objectives or themes from the why questions.

 Themes and objectives: Money and profits are key themes, along with customer satisfaction. Therefore, our objective is to increase the winnings of the dealer while satisfying the customers. If we increase the winnings of the dealer, the casino will bring in more money, and more money will turn into additional profit.

Step 3: Brainstorm and prioritize: What could improve job performance?

 Brainstorming with experienced blackjack dealers produced the following list of possible improvement tasks or activities:

1. Speed up dealer shuffling of cards
2. Speed up dealer dealing of cards
3. Increase dealer's ability to deal with customers
4. Mechanize card shuffling
5. Train the dealer in probability theory to improve knowledge
6. Add another chair to the table
7. Provide more room for players
8. Shorten time dealer is on duty
9. Use only dealers with three or more years of experience

10. Increase the number of card decks used (from one to six decks)
11. Serve more drinks to players

Our dealers and management selected 1, 2, 5, and 6 as the most suitable and effective methods for improving employee performance.

Step 4: Determine countermeasures to meet objectives.

1. Speed up dealer's shuffling the cards.
   Method: Practicing and coaching from a professional.
2. Speed up dealing the cards.
   Method: Practicing and coaching from a professional.
3. Improve dealer's knowledge of probability.
   Method: Education in statistics probability, practice and then observed, and coached by a professional.
4. Add another chair.
   Method: Have industrial engineer study the ergonomics of adding one more chair for an additional player and figure out best arrangement.

Step 5: Validate and identify CSFs.

The improvement ideas and methods were shown and discussed with the blackjack dealers who have produced the desired winnings consistently. These dealers agreed that they were good improvements and will, when implemented, have a high probability of achieving the objective.

The CSFs were then discussed with the dealers to ensure their validity. Each focused on criticality, or the degree to which they were critical to improving job performance. The CSFs selected by the dealers were:

Technical

- Obtaining a coach that can teach the fundamentals needed for improvement
- Selecting and taking the right statistical course

Typical management-related items

- Top management commitment/support
- Employee involvement and commitment
- Communication
- Resources

Identify CSFs, Measure, Track, and Take Action

Step 1: Identify the CSFs. The six CSFs for improving the blackjack dealer's performance were a coach for shuffling and dealing, increasing of probability theory, top management support, employee involvement and commitment, communication, and resources.

Step 2: Measuring the CSFs. As we saw in Chapter 4, CSFs can be measured in several ways. You'll recall from measurement method 1 that top management support, employee involvement and commitment, communications, and resources can be measured by identifying the ascending levels of achievement from 1 to 5.

How will the casino measure the coaching and statistical knowledge CSFs?

These particular CSFs are likely to have the biggest direct impact on the blackjack dealer's overall performance. Timing the dealing and shuffling before and after the CSFs are implemented would provide a good measure of improvement.

And obviously, if more money is coming into the casino once the CSFs have been put into place, then we can count their implementation as successful.

Another way to measure the success of the coaching is assessing client satisfaction (before and after coaching). To determine the success of the blackjack dealer's professional development in statistical knowledge, we can measure that knowledge pre- and post-probability theory training. In addition, to determine dealer effectiveness, dealers could be observed and graded on errors made when shuffling or dealing the cards, accepting late bets, or paying winners incorrectly. Of course, dealers would need to be evaluated both pre- and post-CSF, to determine degree of improvement.

Steps 3 and 4: Track and take action. Track and monitor the measures periodically. In our blackjack dealer example, it could be daily; in other situations, you might monitor the measures weekly, biweekly, or monthly. Take corrective action if needed, and reward and reinforce good performance. For example, if the dealers' shuffling and dealing speeds aren't quick enough, have the coach figure out how to improve both, and then do it. If the dealers' probability theory knowledge isn't sufficient, find out which areas are lacking and provide targeted enhanced training/education. Once our dealer has reached the targets and some time has passed, measurement will no longer be necessary. By then, our dealer will have incorporated the improvements into his or her daily performance period. We'll still need to do periodic money checks and other measurements to ensure that our gains are being maintained.

Example: Military Recruiter

Why is it so important to continually monitor and adjust your CSFs? Because in life, situations and conditions change. When that happens, your CSFs will need to be adjusted or, in some cases, completely changed. As an example, let's look at the conditions in army recruiting, which have changed significantly over the past several years, for a number of reasons.

In 2005, the Government Accountability Office (GAO) noted that recruiters' methods are sometimes too aggressive, and sometimes even criminal.[13]

Why?
Trying to get recruits for Iraq   Good civilian job market (at the time)
                                                    Tough monthly goals

What have some of these recruiters done?
- Resorted to strong-arm tactics
- Harassment
- Falsified documents

How big is the problem?
Military recruiting program: 22,000 people cost more than $1.50 billion a year (see Figure 9.3 for more details). There are 14,000 front-line recruiters who must enlist 2 recruits per month.

Under the military's present recruiting method, what is the driving critical success factor? Performance, determined by whether the recruiter signs up two or more recruits each month. Should that CSF be changed? If so, what is the probability of success in signing up new recruits? The military needs a lot of recruits, especially during wartime. (In January 2007, the president raised the troop levels by over 80,000, greater than 60,000 army and approximately 20,000 marines.) The two-recruit-per-month CSF will probably

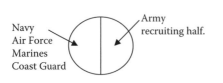

Reviewing problems
from Army, who need
80,000 recruits per year.

	2004	2005
*Failure to Follow Rules	400	630
Criminal Case	30	70

*Military don't track. Some
instances may go unreported

Figure 9.3   Army recruiting data.

remain, with the number per month increased to accommodate the raised ceiling unless a draft (not probable) is approved by Congress. But could a new CSF or emphasis help? The GAO says yes. New recruits should be able to pass boot camp and go on to serve in the military. In other words, army should not recruit anyone that cannot pass the rigorous boot camp simply to meet recruitment targets.

So are potential recruits willing to sign up, and can they pass boot camp? Given the need for new recruits, standards for joining had been lessened. Already, the maximum age had gone from 37 to 42. The army had taken some high school dropouts, some even with existing legal problems, and those with increased body fat. The army collects information such as high school diploma, test scores, physical conditioning, height and weight, etc. If this information is analyzed and standards established, recruits meeting the standards would most likely pass boot camp.

What should be the compelling CSF in this situation? It could be similar to a measure that consultants use. They know that to receive a certain amount of new contracts, they have to bid on a much higher number of contracts. This is their "win" measure of success. To recruit more people, the recruiters are going to need to meet, talk, and discuss service with a higher number of eligible recruits. This will be the driving CSF needed. The number of recruits per month will remain the critical level of success. Action plans to meet more eligible recruits will need to be developed and executed if the recruiting effort is to be successful. It will not be easy to meet or exceed the goals with some universities not letting recruiters on campus, protests by students at some universities against the recruiting efforts, and the increase in troops in Iraq in February–March 2007. Other countermeasures, such as increasing the number of recruits via increased and enhanced TV advertising, were started. It was an objective. New countermeasures were needed. It was vital to our nation.

Now, here we are in 2009. Both wars are still going and the United States still needs new recruits. How have things changed? For one thing, the wars don't seem as dangerous to some people as before. The most significant change is the lack of job opportunity at home for young high school graduates and college graduates. All services, including the army, are having no problem in getting sufficient new recruits. In fact, the age limit has gone back down to 37 years and the education level has risen in the new army. No longer are people with problems recruited. Today, recruiters have no problem meeting their quotas. The critical service level is no longer a concern. Now the emphasis is on ensuring that all possible recruits understand the advantages of service. CSFs to meet recruiting goals are not needed.

CSFs are helpful when we are stretching to meet an objective or goal. If we are not, then setting excellent standards and ensuring they are met becomes the right focus. What happens if the economy significantly recovers? If that happens, then the recruiters will have to address the situation, using the processes I've outlined throughout this book, and develop compelling new CSFs that will help them achieve their recruiting goals.

Chapter 10

CSFs for Individuals

From birth to death, we all go through various stages. At birth to two years of age, we learn to walk. Some learn to talk (at least to a degree), we all learn to signal when we need food or drink, and other behaviors begin to form. From two to five, we continue to grow, learn, talk, and increase our vocabulary. We enter kindergarten to start the formal learning process. Our education continues until the end of high school, after which many will go on to college and graduate programs. Our social skills, religious beliefs, values, and principles grow continuously during this time. Next, we enter our moneymaking years. We gain training, experience, and probably hold three to five jobs in a fifteen- to twenty-five-year period.

We face many challenges during this time. Some develop small businesses, most job hunt, and many marry. Some play sports such as golf, softball, etc. Others hunt, fish, swim, and participate in other sports. Each of us is a unique individual, but we experience many similar things in life. Think back to what we've learned about CSFs in each of the preceding chapters. How many of your own pursuits—in work, or sports, or in your relationships—could CSFs help guide?

Someone once said we have four stages in life: (1) we believe in Santa Claus, (2) we don't believe in Santa Claus, (3) we are Santa Claus, and (4) we look like Santa Claus. In each stage, our CSFs will probably be different. Whatever they are, they can help us be successful if we use the CSF achievement model.

On a Christmas Eve night, when our relatives came to our house for dinner and opening presents, my grandson, Don Jr., who was eight years old at the time, asked his dad and me, "How does Santa know if every boy is good or bad?" Don Sr. answered, "He has a giant crystal ball that observes all little children and knows if they are good or bad."

As I listened to their conversation unfold, I silently wondered what is critical to Santa in accomplishing his mission. Knowing what every boy and girl wants for Christmas, I concluded. He must have a complete *communications system* that enables him to do this. His system enables him to observe children, talk to them on his lap at Christmastime, make notes, check them twice, and conduct myriad behind-the-scenes activities to make it all happen.

Donald said, "Dad, can he deliver everything in his sled at night on Christmas?" Don Sr. answered, "Yes. He has a very special sled that flies like a jet plane through all kinds of weather, pulled by magical reindeer, who are led by one with a nose that is bright." Donald said, "Rudolph!" His dad said, "That's right." So, I thought, Santa must have a *transportation system* that can fly through all kinds of weather safely and accurately to deliver all the toys to their recipients. Donald said, "Where do all the toys come from?" His dad said, "Santa has a *workshop* where all year long the Christmas elves work hard to *produce the toys* that boys and girls want for Christmas." Certainly, I thought, they must have quality control by Santa to make sure they are produced correctly and with quality and below or on cost. Of course, producing the right toys in the right amount is critical to Santa accomplishing his mission.

Donald was happy: he had dreams in his mind of what Santa would bring him and his brother Ricky tomorrow morning! I thought to myself, "What else is critical to Santa accomplishing his mission of delivering toys to little boys and girls for and on Christmas?" His *image,* of course. He must have the red and white suit with cap, white whiskers, a big belly, and a ho-ho-ho laugh that makes that belly shake. Therefore, for Santa to achieve his mission, four CSFs must occur and be executed properly: he needs a comprehensive communications system, a terrific transportation system, a wonderful toy production system with a workplace and elves to accomplish the work, and he needs to maintain his image. Tomorrow, Donald will see all of this come together when he wakes up and runs with his brother into the living room and looks by the Christmas tree. Santa will not let him down. All four CSFs will have been achieved and Santa's customers, my two good and wonderful grandsons, will be excited and very pleased.

Opportunities to Use CSFs

Opportunities to use CSFs are tremendous. CSFs can help you start a business, develop a career progression plan, romance and select a spouse, and on and on.

Use CSFs in your own life to:

■ Prepare for higher-level jobs
■ Start a small business
■ Improve your knowledge and education, etc.

Normally, most of us buy at least one house during our lifetime. Let's see if CSFs occur in that adventure and initiative.

Example: Buying a House

A couple plans to buy a house. There are many decisions to be made and activities to accomplish. First, they need to ensure that they are financially ready. If not, then they need to start taking actions to become so. At least one, if not both, of them must have a job so that their total income is sufficient to get the house they desire. Their credit must be good if they are to get a mortgage with a decent interest rate. Therefore, having jobs with sufficient income and maintaining an acceptable credit score are very important in being able to buy a house. *Being financially ready* is a must (a CSF) to buying a house. When the time comes to start shopping for the house, they must decide: Do we need a real estate agent or can we do it on our own? What size house do we want and need? What location should we look in? Planned communities or not? Do we want the architectural styles and house colors controlled by a homeowners association? Do we want a golf course to be close by? How will we know if a house meets our goals? New or used home? Proximity to schools and shopping malls or hospitals? Do we need a thirty-year or fifteen-year loan? Fixed or variable, and what interest rate would we accept?

House hunting can be fun or frustrating, depending on *the number of possible houses available* (another CSF) to buy in your price range, especially if it is a seller's market. There are several activities that have to be done either by the couple or by their real estate agent, including locating houses for sale, arranging the visit, going and looking, and then deciding whether to make a bid. (Of course, how much to offer becomes paramount if they like a particular house.) The couple should check out the community, the schools, hospital(s), and shopping malls prior to presenting a bid to the sellers. *Closing* becomes the next CSF. This CSF includes securing the mortgage, arranging for paying the down payment and closing costs, ensuring that the house is appraised at the purchase price or higher, ensuring the title is clear, and that the closing date and meeting is set. Of course, the couple wants to walk through the house prior to the closing.

Being financially ready, availability of acceptable houses, and *closing* are our three CSFs. Are they measurable? Yes. For being financially ready, total income should be four times the projected monthly house payment (could vary by state, real estate agent, mortgage company, and housing market); credit should be above a certain score (which varies as above for total income, but at least in the 600s). Housing availability could be satisfied with only one house for sale, if it meets all of the couple's requirements. A national average of how many houses a couple looks at prior to buying a house could be used. I prefer locating the communities that meet the buyer's requirements and visiting at least two to three houses in each prior to making a selection. As far as closing, requirements include having a mortgage contract that gives you the desired interest rate, fixed monthly payment, down payment, and number of years to pay, and closes smoothly on an agreed upon date. The couple checks these at various stages, and if a problem arises, they take corrective action to move the process forward. In this case, the three CSFs can be thought of as three phases of a process that they must go through to buy a house.

The possibilities for individuals to use CSFs are endless. They can be used on a weight loss program, improving your skills in a sport, deciding what church to go to, or planning and executing a large wedding. If it is something you desire and set an objective, then CSFs can help you achieve it. Good luck in all of your pursuits, and may the things critical to you be achieved successfully.

Chapter 11

Conclusion

As we've learned throughout this book, CSFs are a valuable tool that can help you achieve higher performance and successfully implement a system or program and manage a project. In addition, you can use CSFs to improve job performance and pursue individual goals.

In today's world of quality improvement, productivity enhancement, Lean thinking, Six Sigma implementation, kaizen events, seven QC (Quality Control) tools, planning tools and techniques, and so on, CSFs have not been used as often as they should. CSFs can be an exciting, beneficial tool if identified by an improvement team, measured, tracked, and monitored, and if corrective actions are taken when needed to ensure that they are fully implemented and achieved.

This book has taken a widely known concept (introduced in 1961), an often misused or misunderstood tool, and shown how it should be a consideration *any* time that you want to improve something in your business or your life.

Although thousands of applications are available on the Internet, it is very difficult to find even one book that explains the process of identifying CSFs and then how to measure their implementation. I wrote this book to fill that void and make CSFs use a practical, simple, and rewarding experience.

If you are going to improve anything, always ask: "What is critical, and what do I need to do to make it happen?" Don't leave improvement or pursuit of excellence or happiness to chance. Good luck in all of your improvement adventures and through all the stages of your life.

Appendix A: Key Result Areas

Key Result Areas	Multivoting	
	1st Vote	2nd Vote
1. Quality		
2. Schedule		
3. Quantity		
4. Service		
5. Cycle time		
6. Cost		
7. People/human resources/respect/motivation		
8. Delivery/timeliness		
9. Organizational responsibility/community relations		
10. Financial strength (cost, profit, market share)		
11. Profit		
12. Professionalism		
13. Management/leadership		
14. Cooperation/communication/coordinations productivity		
15. Quality of work life		
16. Efficiency		
17. Utilization		
18. Morale/attitudes		
19. Safety		

continued

Key Result Areas	Multivoting	
	1st Vote	2nd Vote
20. Throughput		
21. Budgetability		
22. Innovation/creation		
23. Effectiveness		
24. Reliability		
25. Technology		
26. Market share		
27. Mission		
28. Awareness		
29. Image		
30. Organizational structure/streamlining		
31. Performance		
32. Visibility		
33. Customer satisfaction		
34. Business practices		
35. Partnerships		
36. Control		
37. Environment		
38. Value		
39. Cleanliness		
40. Consistency		
41. Virtual		
42. Vision		
43. Value		
44. Security		

Appendix B: Brainstorming

Brainstorming is a technique to encourage creative thinking. The emphasis is first on generating a *quantity* of ideas. Later, through analysis, you'll identify and select the *quality* ideas from the list.

The rules* for using brainstorming are:

- Clearly state purpose.
- In sequence, each person takes a turn.
- One thought at a time.
- Don't criticize ideas; discuss ideas.
- Build on ideas of others.

---

* Reprinted with permission from Actionable Performance Measurement: A Key to Success,
  ASQ Quality Press ©2006 American Society for Quality.

Appendix C: Modified Nominal Group Technique

As we've discussed throughout this book, the modified nominal group technique can be an effective means to identify your CSFs. Below are the goals or objectives*, recommended group size, and settings that you need to have in place to use this technique.

Goals

1. Increase creativity and participation in group meetings involving problem-solving or fact-finding tasks
2. Develop or expand perception of critical issues within problem areas
3. Establish priorities, considering the viewpoints of differently oriented groups
4. Obtain the input of many individuals without unbalanced participation, which often occurs in large groups

Group Size

Five to eight participants is ideal.

---

* Reprinted with permission from Actionable Performance Measurement: A Key to Success, ASQ Quality Press ©2006 American Society for Quality.

Physical Setting

Groups are seated around tables with an easel, a paper pad, and magic markers available. Paper and pencil are furnished to each participant.
  The process is:

1. *Silent generation.* Write the objective on the paper pad so that it's visible to all participants. Without any discussion, each participant should spend approximately ten minutes silently generating lists of ideas relating to the objective. The actual time will vary depending on the scope of the problem or objective under consideration.
2. *Round-robin.* A volunteer in each group acts as a recorder or scribe for that group. He or she asks each participant, one at a time, to present an idea, which that person has listed on a pad or Post-it. The items are recorded on the easel paper pad; if Post-its are used, they can be placed on a whiteboard. This continues until each participant's ideas have been included. Discussion is not allowed, nor should any concern be given to overlap, at this time. "Hitchhiking," by having members generate new ideas on their pads, based on items presented by others, is encouraged. This should take at least ten minutes.
3. *Clarification/discussion.* Groups should now discuss the items on their sheets for purposes of:
   - Clarification
   - Elaboration
   - Additional new items (time depends on scope)
4. *Prioritization/selection.* Next, groups will use multivoting to determine their top priorities, the number of which will vary depending on the objective. Each participant chooses half of the items. During the second vote, participants choose half of the items that receive the highest votes on the first vote, and keep voting in this manner until the group gets to a predetermined desired number. General consensus should be achieved in ten minutes or less.

Appendix D: The Traditional CSF List for Management Initiatives

In my experience, the same forty-two CSFs are commonly used during management improvement initiatives. Normally, you'll identify five to seven of these and use them for each of your improvement efforts or initiatives.

Each CSF can be further broken down into several subfactors. By identifying the subfactors, you can select the best technique to measure the implementation progress of the CSF.

Here are the forty-two CSFs that comprise the traditional list:

1. Accountability
   - Responsible for actions taken, both performance and quality
   - Understands what is expected and strives to achieve
   - Individual is competent in the tasks, job, process, program, etc.; if not, training, experience, and education should be provided
2. Best practices
   - Employees provide input as to best practices they have used or observed
   - Benchmarking—both internal and external
   - Internet research for best methods
   - Best practices recorded and placed in work or process instructions
3. Client relationship
   - Gets along well with clients
   - Understands clients' needs
   - Delivery meets exceptional performance requirement, and clients agree
   - Builds trust
   - When clients need a product or service, they think of you

4. Coaching/facilitating
   - Helping individuals, people, teams, or groups learn a new skill or tool, or follow a process or procedure
   - Passing on best practices or skills
   - Keeping team on track
   - Setting agendas that drive improvement
   - Solving problems
   - Generating issues
   - Learning new tools or techniques
5. Communication
   - Internal communications
   - External communications plan
   - Written news on subject
   - Common language on subject material
   - Speeches on subject
   - Communicating why we are doing this
   - Communicating expectations
   - Providing pertinent facts, including successes and reasons for failure
6. Constancy of purpose
   - Obtaining a focus
   - Staying on course until objectives or visions are achieved
   - From start of an initiative, staying on path or road map to conclusion
7. Continual improvement
   - Uses PDCA (plan-do-check-act) philosophy and keeps turning the wheel (PDCA:PDCA) for continuous improvement
   - Performs management reviews
   - Leadership dedicated, knowledgeable, and challenging
   - Everyone seeks ways to improve operations and processes
8. Cost system
   - Cost accumulation by activity/product/service
   - Cost analysis
   - Cost information is timely, accurate, complete, and accessible; reports can be generated based on information collected
   - Cost-effective system that meets cost data and analysis need
9. Cross-functional management
   - Manages cross-functional areas to improve a process, program, procedure, or system
   - Composition of team is very important; must include members from all-important functions

- Functions as a team although members have different bosses in their chains of command
- Performs best when linked to organization's vision
- Accountable to the organization's top leadership council, team, etc.

10. Customer voice/satisfaction
- Customers' perceptions are greater than their expectations
- Very satisfied or not with product or service
- Customers participate in design of product or observation of service to be provided, through customer panels, customer focus groups, etc.
- Organizations use customers' comments and survey results to improve their processes, strategies, etc.

11. Discipline and consequences
- Competent in duties to perform; has necessary experience, education, and training
- Follows specifications, plans, work instructions, etc.
- Knows risks, takes precautions
- Safety is paramount
- Mistakes are dealt with in fair but appropriate manner

12. Effective change management
- Plan for cultural change, through a plan that includes a vision or policy, training, goals and objectives, measures, employee involvement, executive reviews, etc.
- Develop transition plan that includes communication, informing all involved; provide training if needed, let employees vent, listen to and answer their concerns
- Organizations don't change, people do!

13. Efficiency
- Resources are used as planned
- Measured, tracked, monitored, and corrective action taken if needed
- Targets established
- Measure is kept current and visible to all involved

14. Employee involvement
- Understands objectives, vision, process, etc., and is involved in the improvement of performance
- Trained or educated in what needs to be done
- Possesses sufficient experience and is competent in the tasks/activities involved
- Strives for excellence in performance

- Communicates positively on the program, system, or process being engaged

15. Executive engagement
    - Communicates vision or objectives
    - Gets involved: heads meetings, supports activities, champions the cause, recognizes and rewards achievements
    - Provides leadership and resources

16. Information
    - Sufficient to highlight potential problems
    - Adequate to manage by
    - Timely, accurate, and proper coverage
    - Useful, meaningful, and readily accessible
    - Cost-effective
    - Reproducible

17. Innovation
    - New ideas
    - Creativity
    - Something useful that is new
    - Adapting one area to another to improve or make a better product or service

18. Integrated into daily work
    - The improvement initiative becomes how you do your daily work
    - Embedded into employee behavior, process standards, and is fully integrated into the organization's work and social systems and culture
    - Becomes just the right way to do things

19. Leadership
    - Lead by example
    - Communicate what is important (your vision) at speeches, meetings
    - Support by providing resources
    - Perform constructive executive or management reviews

20. Linkage/strategic alignment
    - Objectives linked to organization's vision, key result areas, and goals
    - If improvement is at one level, then it improves the next higher level to which it is linked
    - Employees have input to the process and importance of linkage is communicated to all involved
    - Lower organizational levels' goals, objectives, systems, processes, etc.; support next higher level

21. Management involvement
    - Approves initiative
    - Communicates benefits
    - Recognizes achievement
    - Breaks down barriers
    - Provides resources
    - Easy to talk with
22. Management review
    - Top management in team composition
    - Meets periodically
    - Agenda established early
    - Team members, whose work is being reviewed, are present
    - Asks question to ensure adequacy, suitability, and effectiveness
    - Drives continuous improvement
23. Measurement
    - Actionable performance indicators (meaningful, provides adequate coverage, cost-effective, measurable, and graphed)
    - Data collection plan for each indicator
    - Targets or standards established
    - Indicators kept current and visible
    - Readily accessible to people needing the information
24. Objectives and targets
    - Objectives are established
    - Made SMART (specific, measurable, actionable, relevant, and time framed)
    - Realistic, but stretch targets, limits, or standards are established
    - Actions identified, that if done, will achieve the objective(s)
    - Linked to objectives, goals, key result areas, or vision
    - A champion or accountable, responsible person assigned to each objective
    - Action plans developed
25. Productivity
    - To improve productivity $= \dfrac{\text{output}}{\text{input}}$ or $\dfrac{\text{quality output}}{\text{input}}$
    - More output, less input
    - Covers process, work instructions, elements of a system, etc.
    - If followed, results are what are desired
    - Ensure standards, including work and safety, are achieved if right materials, equipment, work plan, and competent personnel are provided

26. Projects
    - Person(s) responsible identified (project manager)
    - Purpose, objective, or why developed
    - Activities to accomplish identified and resources needed
    - *Who* is going to do it, *when*, *where*, and *how*
    - Create a Gantt chart, with activities time framed, milestones described, and start to end identified
    - Progress reviews
    - Contingency plans
    - Criticality defined
    - Ensure linkage to goals
    - Replicate if possible and feasible
27. Proven methodology
    - Use a proven methodology, such as strategic or ISO 14001 environmental management system—a structured process that leads to a desired action or state
    - Can be used by a team
    - May need facilitation to achieve objectives
28. Quality
    - Meets requirements or specifications
    - Accomplishes the purpose or does the job
    - No rework
    - On time, within cost, safe, and functions as intended
29. Recognition/rewards
    - Recognize achievements and efforts
    - Must be sincere, appropriate, and timely
    - Rewards commensurate with achievements
    - Leadership (top management and managers) should be involved
    - Communication of recognitions/rewards should be done by several media (letters, staff meeting, recognition events, newsletters, etc.)
30. Resources
    - Sufficient to accomplish the project(s) or achieve the objectives
    - Timely and useful
    - Managed (project management) and efficiently utilized or consumed
31. Roles and responsibilities
    - Defined
    - Understood
    - Pursued
    - Accountabilities established

- Reviews of performance
- Published or readily available
- Communicated throughout organizations
- Appropriate person is capable of accomplishing

32. Safety
    - Safe
    - Safety program in being
    - Accidents, incidents, doctor calls, etc., measured, tracked, root causes identified, countermeasures taken and communicated
    - Safe best practices being used in all work situations
    - Safety training provided
    - Workers assessed as to competence skills, education, training, and attitude
    - Safety promoted at workbench meetings, staff meetings, stand-up meetings, etc.
    - Audits, walkthroughs, observations performed periodically
    - Accidents investigated to determine root cause(s) and preventive measures put in place

33. Salesmanship
    - Able to sell:
        - Customers
        - Management
        - Employees
        - Regulators
    - Develop sales plan
    - Train salesmen; role-play techniques and principles
    - Develop best practices and use
    - Evaluate and improve sales capability
    - Motivate, recognize, and award salesmen

34. Stewardship
    - Managers show pride and involvement
    - Accepts ownership of process, product, service, etc.
    - Pride in making sure it is done right, with quality, and on time

35. Teaming
    - Team size—six to eight members preferred; ten or under a must
    - Teams chartered for a reason (mission or purpose defined)
    - Team composition must be representative of what is to be done
    - Type of team selected for the job to be done

- Progress rapidly through Tuckman's four stages (form, storm, norm, and perform)
- Teams jelled to work on a problem (team building, teamwork, synergy)
- Team members supportive of each other
- Objective, listen, participate; committed team members
- High performance—little conflict and focused
- Trained in the tools or techniques needed to accomplish the mission or solve the problem
- Follow a structured process to solve a problem or meet the objective
- Have effective team leaders, facilitators, and involved team members

36. Technology
    - New
    - Improved
    - Cost-effective
    - Does the job quicker, better, and with quality
    - Easy to use
    - Safe and efficient

37. Training
    - Specific: Details what is needed to accomplish a task, process, or solve a problem
    - Tools or techniques needed to accomplish the objective—job, task, process, action plan, solve a problem, etc.
    - Training for team leaders, facilitators, team members; process improvement, reengineering process, strategic planning, Lean manufacturing, Six Sigma, black belt, green belt, yellow belt, team and statistics group dynamics, and measurement are examples for improvement training; will vary depending on organization's needs; generally, starts with awareness training (broad and overview) and then gets specific (how to accomplish specific tasks, use a tool, or technique)

38. Values
    - Guiding principles to fall back on that come from culture, education, experiences, and beliefs
    - Doing what is right
    - Organizational conscience

39. Value added
    - Supports the mission or objective
    - If not accomplished, it will cause a problem
    - A necessary activity, process, or function
    - Missed if not present

40. Winning
    - Achieving goals or objectives
    - Beating the competition
    - Advancing toward world class or best in class
    - A feeling of achievement

Appendix E: The CSF Method

Major Activity	Subactivities
1. Define purpose and scope	1. Determine if the factor is organization-wide or for a subunit, such as a business unit, a region, a district or division.
	2. Determine whether or not it is a strategic thrust needed to achieve the mission, or a separate improvement initiative such as Six Sigma, Lean office, reengineering, process improvement, etc.
	3. Establish a team with knowledgeable members and a strong team leader.
2. Collect data	1. Perform a document review of strategic plans, vision, mission statements, goals, objectives, performance measures, business plans, organization charts, and other related documents.
	2. Develop an interview plan, including participant questions, and prepare for the interview.
	3. Conduct interviews in two to three sessions, as needed, and summarize data. First session, identify mission, goals, objectives, future plans, and possible CSFs and performance measures. Conduct second and third interviews as needed to review findings and validate adequacy.
3. Evaluate data	1. Develop activity statements.
	2. Perform affinity groupings of the activity statements or identify appropriate KRAs.
	3. Develop summary themes or use KRAs to group relevant activities by KRA.
4. Identify CSFs	1. From summary themes or KRAs, identify possible CSFs.

continued

Major Activity	Subactivities
5. Analyze CSFs	1. Determine comparison criteria and analyze CSF vs. goals, objectives, functions, etc., or ask, "If the CSFs are achieved, will we achieve the KRA?" Then, "If the CSFs are achieved, did they achieve the desired objective?"
	2. Using a comparison matrix or relationship diagram, analyze and understand the CSFs and their relationship to each other.

Glossary

Affinity diagram or affinity groupings: A technique to organize a multitude of ideas or items into homogeneous groupings so that themes or representative headings can be identified.[4]

Benchmarking: Identify a process and process metric to improve by analyzing a similar organization or one that does a world-class function. It could also be an internal group.[11]

Champion: A middle or top manager accountable to lead a major effort, such as obtaining a goal or achieving an objective.

Critical-to-success factors (CSFs): Rockart[1] defined CSFs in several ways: "key areas of activity in which favorable results are absolutely necessary to reach goals"; "factors that are critical to the success of the organization"; "key areas of activities that should receive constant and careful attention from management"; "key areas where things must go right for the business to flourish"; "a relatively few number of important factors which a manager should focus attention."

Critical-to-success measures: Indicators that must be at a certain value for the endeavor to be a success.

CSF achievement model: Identifying CSFs, selecting CSFs, measuring CSFs, tracking and checking, and taking corrective action (if needed).

CSF method: A technique invented at MIT's Sloan School, by John Rockart, to assist businesses in creating CSFs to enable success in accomplishing their mission and objectives. The method starts with a vision and mission statement and proceeds to CSFs for an organization or for a subcomponent such as a region, business unit, or division.[1]

eBay: An Internet auction company where individuals sell their products and buyers can easily purchase them. Anyone can sell or buy providing they follow eBay rules.

Environmental scan: A look at government, economy, technology, and other changes that could occur in the near future.

External forces: Changes in policies, procedures, laws, etc., that can impact an organization.

Fishbone diagram: A cause-and-effect diagram that enables an individual or a team to identify possible causes that lead to the problem (the effect). Looks like a fish swimming to the right.[10]

Goals: A statement of what an organization wants to achieve that is broad and long range.[7]

Green lighting: In brainstorming, everyone has slowed down with their ideas, and the floor is then opened up to anyone to offer an idea (do not have to go in rotation).

Implementation measurement method: Uses a 1 to 5 scale, with 1 representing getting started and 5 meaning fully achieved. The state of implementation is written for each level and for each selected CSF. The team assesses implementation progress periodically and uses the information to plan for higher levels of implementation.

ISO: International Organization for Standardization (www.iso.org). A standards organization based in Switzerland that coordinates development of standards (process, environmental, etc.) for worldwide use.

Key result areas (KRAs): Those areas of an organization that will yield the most improvement if they receive resources. Examples are productivity, quality, efficiency, and customer satisfaction.[7]

Method: A particular way of doing a defined amount of work that includes all material, tools, equipment or other resources, such as people, to accomplish.

Nominal group technique: An idea generation technique consisting of silent generation of ideas, making ideas visible, clarifying and combining, prioritizing, and selecting the best ideas.[10]

Objectives: A statement to improve an activity or process that is specific, measurable, actionable, relevant, and time framed. It is short range, for one to two years.[7]

Performance measures: A metric or measure of a key element, objective, process, result, or outcome that includes a graph, target, formula of the measure, and data collection plan.[7]

Process: A sequence of activities that produce a product, service, or information.

Relationship diagram: A diagram that shows a relationship by drawing a line with the arrow pointed toward the element being impacted.[4]

Strategy: A course of action to favorably impact or improve a strategic objective and its corresponding performance measure.[14]

SWOT analysis: Used in strategic planning. An organization develops its strengths, weaknesses, opportunities, and threats. Next, it uses the strengths to offset weaknesses and to select opportunities for improvement.

Team: A group of people assigned to solve a problem or improve a process or method.

Traditional list (TL): A list, developed by the author, of CSFs commonly used or evident in management improvement initiatives. See Appendix D.

Vision: Senior management or site management, through analysis and using the customer's voice, determines where they want the organization to be in the long term (five to twenty years).

References

1. Rockart, J. F. 1986. A primer on critical success factors. In *Rise of managerial computing*. Homewood, IL: Dow Jones, Irwin.
2. Hox, A. C., and Majluf, N. S. 1983. The use of the industry attractiveness—Business strength matrix in strategic planning. *Interfallen B*, No. 2, April.
3. Caralli, R. A. 2004. *The critical success factor method: Establishing a foundation for enterprise security management*. Pittsburgh, PA: Carnegie Mellon Software Engineering Institute.
4. Mizuno, S., ed. 1988. Management for quality improvement. In *The 7 new QC tools*. Cambridge, MA: Productivity Press 4:89–114.
5. Rockart, J. F., and Bullen, C. V. 1981. *A primer on critical success factors*. Cambridge, MA: Center for Information Systems Research, Sloan School of Management, Massachusetts Institute of Technology.
6. Chang Kae, H. 1987. *Management critical success factors*. Weiston, MA: Allyn and Bacon, Inc.
7. Howell, M. T. 2005. *Actionable performance measurement—A key to success*. Milwaukee, WI: ASQ Quality Press.
8. James, B. 1982–1988. *The Bill James abstract*. New York: Ballantine Books.
9. Chang, R. Y., and Morgan, M. 2000. *Performance score cards: Measuring the right things in the real world*. San Francisco: Jossey-Bass.
10. Mears, P. 1995. *Quality improvement tools and techniques*. New York: McGraw Hill.
11. Camp, R. C. 1989. *Benchmarking: Finding and implementing best practices that lead to superior performance*. Milwaukee, WI: ASQC Quality Press.
12. Dickerson, J. 2006. Improve product development using IPD. *Quality Progress ASQ*, p. 96.
13. *Dallas Morning News*, August 15, 2006, p. 2A. http://www.dallasnews.com/sharedcontent/dws/news/nation/stories/081056dnnatmilitaryrecruit.21353b2.html#.
14. Digman, L. A. 1986. *Strategic management: Concepts, decisions, cases*. Plano, TX: Business Publications, Inc.

Suggested Reading

Bergeron, F., and Begin, C. 1989. The use of critical success factors in review of information system, a case study. *Journal of Management Information Systems* 5:111–24.

Boynton, A. C., and Zmud, R. W. 1984. An assessment of critical success factors. *Sloan Management Review* 25:17–27.

Daniel, D. R. 1961. Management information crisis. *Harvard Business Review*, September–October.

Drucker, P. F. 1964. *Managing for results*. New York: Harper and Row.

Huotani, M.-L., and Wilson, T. D. 1996. The value chain, CSFs and company information needs in two Finnish companies. In *Information science: Integration in perspective*, ed. P. Ingwersen and P. Niels Ole, 311–23. Copenhagen: The Royal School of Librarianship.

Huotani, M.-L., and Wilson, T. D. 2001. Determining organizational information needs: The CSFs approach. *Information Research*.

Leidecker, J. K., and Bruno, A. V. 1984. Identifying and using CSFs. *Long Range Planning* 17:23–32.

Pollalis, Y. A., and Freze, I. A. 1993. A new look at CSFs. *Information Strategy*, pp. 24–34.

Rockhart, J. F. 1979. Chief executives define their own data needs. *Harvard Business Review*, March–April, p. 57.2.

Steiner, G. A. 1979. *Strategic planning*. New York: MacMillan.

Index

About the Author

Marvin Howell is a senior environmental associate with Analytical Services, Inc. He is a government contractor with duties and responsibilities for developing, implementing, and maintaining an ISO-14001-based environmental management system (EMS) program at two analytical laboratories, an air wing, a field division, and several other government facilities. He has more than fifteen years experience in the environmental field with four years of EMS experience in the areas of development and implementation within federal government agencies.

Howell was director and president of Quality Management Technologies, Inc. of Miami, Florida for ten years. The main mission of the international company was to perform industrial engineering projects and implement quality improvement efforts to include strategic planning, process improvement (including Six Sigma and Lean), team building, and team performance. His clients included some USAF squadrons, centers, and commands, Intel, Florida Power and Light Company (FPL), and others. He has extensive experience in new construction, facility maintenance, reliability, strategic planning and measurement, and environmental and quality improvement.

Howell served in the USAF civil engineering in numerous engineering, management, and human resources assignments and retired as a lieutenant colonel.

He also worked at FPL in numerous areas as a supervising management analyst, reliability engineer, and project manager, and as manager of the Distribution Planning and Reliability Department. Howell was instrumental in assisting FPL's successful pursuit of the Deming Quality Prize from Japan.

He is a published author on performance measurement; *Actionable Performance Measurement—A Key to Success* was published in 2005 by ASQ. He received his MS industrial engineering degree from the University of Pittsburgh and a BS degree in mechanical engineering from Mississippi State University. He is a professional engineer.